Cryptocurrency Investing for Beginners

The Ultimate 30-Day Step-by-Step Guide to Easily & Safely Invest in Crypto, Build Wealth, and Avoid Costly Mistakes—Even if You're Starting from Zero

Arthur Bell

Contents

Introduction

I still remember the day I met a young man who turned my world upside down.

He was 23, brimming with energy and enthusiasm, and had just made a million dollars in crypto. It was like hearing a modern-day fairy tale.

But this wasn't magic—this was real.

That conversation lit a fire in me. It was the spark I needed to dive into the world of cryptocurrency.

With his guidance, I opened an account on a reputable exchange and bought my first cryptocurrency.

Fast forward a few years, I've had multiple coins that have over quadrupled in value, and my net worth has climbed dramatically thanks to crypto.

Now, I want to share everything I've learned with you.

This book is your step-by-step guide to confidently investing in cryptocurrency.

It's designed for beginners who want clear, practical advice. We will break down everything you need to know into simple, actionable steps.

You won't find complicated jargon or overwhelming information here. Instead, you'll get the tools to understand and thrive in the crypto market.

Cryptocurrency is no longer just a buzzword. It's becoming an essential part of today's financial landscape.

Last year alone, the market grew exponentially, with new investors entering the space daily.

People are seeing the potential for real financial independence.

Cryptocurrency offers opportunities that traditional markets can't.

Whether diversifying your portfolio or seeking alternative investment avenues, crypto is transforming the way we think about finance and investment.

Whether you're young, eager, and tech-savvy or older and looking for new ways to grow your wealth, this book is for you.

My goal is to demystify the complexities of cryptocurrency investing and make it accessible to everyone, regardless of age or experience.

Here's what you can expect to learn in this book.

We'll start with setting up your crypto wallet and choosing the correct exchange.

Then, we'll dive into how to buy your first coins and the importance of market trends.

I'll guide you through reading charts and making informed decisions.

You'll also learn how to protect your investments from scams.

By the end, you'll have a holistic view of cryptocurrency investing.

Our promise is simple: follow this guide, and it will equip you to start investing in crypto, build wealth, and avoid costly mistakes.

Even if you're starting from zero, you'll find the information you need to succeed.

What makes this book unique?

I've included a glossary of terms to familiarize you with the industry language.

You'll find a chapter on bot trading, offering insights into automated strategies.

We'll also explore the BTC Rainbow Chart, breaking down what it means and how you can use it to make smarter investment decisions.

These elements set this book apart from other beginner guides.

I invite you to join me on this 30-day journey. Together, we'll explore the exciting world of cryptocurrency.

By the end, you'll have the knowledge and confidence to invest successfully.

So grab a coffee, settle in, and let's get started. Your crypto adventure awaits.

Laying the Foundation

Have you ever wondered what it feels like to hold the future in the palm of your hand? That's the sensation I had when I first bought cryptocurrency.

It was as if I'd unlocked a door to a new era of finance, one that didn't play by the old rules.

This chapter sets the stage for your adventure into the digital currency world.

We'll cover the essentials—the nuts and bolts of cryptocurrency—to ensure you have a solid understanding before investing.

You'll learn the "how" and the "why" behind cryptocurrency's existence and its growing role in today's financial systems.

This foundation will be your roadmap, guiding you through the complexities of the crypto market with confidence.

Cryptocurrency 101: Understanding Digital Assets

Cryptocurrency is an entirely new kind of money. Instead of being physical like cash or coins, it's entirely digital and protected by advanced coding to keep it secure.

Unlike traditional money created and controlled by governments or central banks (like the Federal Reserve), cryptocurrencies work through a **decentralized network**.

This means no single organization, like a bank, is in charge.

Instead, cryptocurrencies run on a system called **blockchain technology**.

A blockchain is like a giant, shared notebook that keeps track of every transaction.

This notebook is stored across many computers worldwide, so no one person or group has total control.

This setup makes cryptocurrencies independent, which is both a powerful advantage and a unique challenge.

One of the unique characteristics of cryptocurrencies is their security.

Cryptography, the science of encoding and decoding information, ensures that transactions are secure and private.

Each transaction is recorded on a blockchain, a digital ledger open for everyone to see, ensuring transparency and trust.

This ledger is immutable—once a transaction is recorded, it cannot be altered or deleted.

This makes cryptocurrencies resistant to fraud and hacking, although they are not entirely immune to cyber threats.

Another defining feature is peer-to-peer transactions. With cryptocurrency, you can transfer funds directly to another person without an intermediary like a bank.

This can significantly reduce transaction costs and increase speed, especially for international transfers.

Imagine sending money across the globe in minutes without the hefty fees charged by traditional banks—that's the power of cryptocurrency.

This especially benefits those in countries with unstable currencies or restrictive banking systems.

Cryptocurrencies also promote financial inclusion by providing access to financial services for the unbanked—those who don't have access to traditional banking.

Using a smartphone allows anyone to participate in the cryptocurrency market, opening up opportunities for economic empowerment.

Cryptocurrencies are also disrupting traditional banking practices. They challenge the status quo by eliminating the need for intermediaries in financial transactions.

This potential for disruption is forcing financial institutions to rethink their roles and adapt to new technologies.

As you begin your journey into cryptocurrency investing, you'll encounter a few key terms. Understanding these will help you navigate the crypto landscape with ease.

For instance, a **"coin"** refers to a digital currency that operates independently on its own blockchain, like Bitcoin.

A **"token,"** on the other hand, is a digital asset issued on another blockchain, such as Ethereum.

You'll also need to know about private keys and public addresses.

Your **private key** is like a password that unlocks your cryptocurrency wallet, while your **public address** is like an email address where others can send you cryptocurrency.

And then there's **blockchain** itself, the technology underpinning cryptocurrencies, which we'll explore in depth later.

Using cryptocurrency comes with its own set of benefits and challenges.

On the plus side, cryptocurrencies offer anonymity and privacy, as transactions don't require personal information.

However, this anonymity can also be a double-edged sword, raising concerns about illicit activities.

The volatility of cryptocurrencies is another challenge. Prices can fluctuate wildly, making them risky investments.

Yet, this volatility can also lead to significant gains.

Regulatory hurdles add another layer of complexity. Governments are still figuring out how to regulate cryptocurrencies, which can lead to legal uncertainties.

Cryptocurrency is a fascinating, complex world with the potential to revolutionize finance as we know it.

As you continue through this book, you'll gain a deeper understanding of how to navigate this new landscape, build wealth, and avoid the common pitfalls that catch many beginners off guard.

The Evolution of Cryptocurrency: A Brief History

The story of cryptocurrency begins with the quest for digital cash. This concept intrigued computer scientists and cryptographers for decades.

As early as the 1980s and 90s, visionaries imagined a world where money could exist online, independent of banks and governments.

The idea was to create a virtual currency that mimicked the properties of physical cash, allowing people to exchange value directly without intermediaries.

This dream was primarily driven by the pioneers of cryptography, who were exploring ways to secure digital transactions using complex mathematical algorithms.

Their work laid the groundwork for what was to come, setting the stage for a financial revolution.

Enter **Bitcoin**, the first successful cryptocurrency and the brainchild of an enigmatic figure—or perhaps a group—known as **Satoshi Nakamoto**.

In 2008, Nakamoto published a white paper titled "Bitcoin: A Peer-to-Peer Electronic Cash System."

This document outlined a revolutionary way to conduct transactions over the internet, free from centralized control.

Bitcoin was officially launched in 2009, marking the start of a new era in finance.

The first-ever Bitcoin transaction occurred in January 2009, when Nakamoto sent ten Bitcoins to a developer named Hal Finney, one of the earliest adopters of this groundbreaking technology.

This simple act was the genesis of a movement that would grow exponentially over the next decade.

As Bitcoin gained traction, the crypto market began to diversify by introducing alternative cryptocurrencies that sought to improve upon or differentiate from Bitcoin's model.

These were called **altcoins**.

Among the most notable is **Ethereum**, introduced in 2015 by a young visionary named **Vitalik Buterin**.

Ethereum brought **smart contracts** into the mix, enabling automated, self-executing contracts with terms directly written into code.

This innovation expanded the potential uses of blockchain technology beyond simple transactions, paving the way for **decentralized applications** or **dApps**.

Another early altcoin, **Litecoin**, aimed to be the "silver" to Bitcoin's "gold."

Launched in 2011, Litecoin offered faster transaction times and a slightly different encryption algorithm, appealing to users who sought a quicker, more efficient alternative.

The cryptocurrency journey is dotted with significant milestones that have shaped its trajectory and public perception.

One of the earliest and most notorious events was the collapse of the Mt. Gox exchange in 2014, which, at its height, handled over 70% of all Bitcoin transactions.

The hack resulted in the loss of hundreds of thousands of Bitcoins, shaking the confidence of investors and highlighting the vulnerabilities in the nascent crypto infrastructure.

Despite this setback, the crypto world soldiered on, reaching a fever pitch during the **Initial Coin Offering (ICO)** boom of 2017.

ICOs allowed startups to raise funds by issuing their own tokens, leading to a surge of new projects and, unfortunately, a fair share of scams.

This boom eventually led to a crash, as regulatory scrutiny increased and many tokens lost value rapidly.

Yet, amidst the turbulence, cryptocurrencies continued to gain legitimacy and acceptance.

Major companies began to explore blockchain technology and its potential applications.

For instance, financial giants like JPMorgan and tech behemoths like IBM started integrating blockchain into their operations, recognizing its potential to enhance security, transparency, and efficiency.

In some jurisdictions, governments began to legalize and regulate cryptocurrencies, providing a framework for their use and fostering greater trust among consumers and investors.

The evolution of cryptocurrency reflects human ingenuity and the relentless pursuit of innovation.

While it has faced challenges and controversies, it continues to push the boundaries of what's possible in the financial world.

As we look ahead, the lessons learned from Bitcoin's inception, the rise of altcoins, and the industry's growing pains will undoubtedly inform the future of digital currency.

We stand on the brink of a new financial paradigm that promises to redefine how we think about and use money.

Blockchain Basics: The Technology Behind Cryptocurrency

At the core of cryptocurrency lies blockchain technology, a marvel of modern computing that has transformed how we think about data and transactions.

Imagine a blockchain as a digital ledger, a collection of records called **blocks** linked together in a single list or **chain**.

Each block contains a list of transactions, and once a block is filled, it is closed and cryptographically secured to the previous one, creating a secure, unchangeable chain of data.

This continuous chain ensures that data entered into the blockchain remains there permanently, creating a trustworthy record that is practically impossible to alter without detection.

A crucial component of blockchain technology is its consensus mechanism, which ensures that all network participants agree on the ledger's contents.

Take **Proof of Work (PoW)**, for example. It requires network participants, called **miners**, to solve complex mathematical puzzles to validate transactions and add them to the blockchain.

This process is resource-intensive but adds a layer of security, making altering past transactions difficult and costly.

On the other hand, **Proof of Stake (PoS)** is a less energy-consuming alternative.

Instead of solving puzzles, validators are chosen based on the number of coins they hold. They are willing to **"stake"** as collateral, encouraging them to act in the network's best interest.

The strength of blockchain technology lies in its distributed nature.

Unlike traditional databases stored on a single server, blockchain data is spread across a network of computers, each holding a copy of the ledger.

This distribution means there is no single point of failure. If one **node** fails or is compromised, the others continue functioning, making the network highly resilient against attacks.

Blockchain maintains integrity and trust through its transparency and immutability. Every transaction recorded on the blockchain is visible to all participants, reducing the chance of fraud.

Once a block is added to the chain, its data is set in stone, providing a permanent and verifiable history of all transactions.

This transparency builds trust among users, as they can independently verify the integrity of the data without relying on a central authority.

Different blockchain architectures serve various purposes.

Public blockchains, like Bitcoin and Ethereum, are open to anyone who wishes to participate.

They are decentralized, allowing users worldwide to join the network, validate transactions, and access the ledger.

Private blockchains, in contrast, restrict access to a select group of participants, often within a single organization.

These benefit companies needing to maintain privacy while leveraging blockchain's advantages.

Permissioned blockchains, a hybrid of public and private, allow specific actions to be performed by approved participants, making them ideal for enterprise solutions like supply chain management, where data accuracy and trust are paramount.

Speaking of supply chains, blockchain's role in this area is transformative.

It offers a transparent, tamper-proof record of every transaction, improving trust and efficiency.

Companies can track products from origin to delivery, ensuring authenticity and reducing fraud.

This has become especially crucial in industries dealing with complex supply chains, where verifying the legitimacy of each step is vital.

Despite its strengths, blockchain is often misunderstood.

One common myth is that blockchain is unhackable.

While the technology is highly secure, vulnerabilities can exist at the application layer or in how people manage their private keys.

Another misconception is that blockchain is just another type of database.

Unlike traditional databases, which are controlled by a central authority, blockchain's decentralized nature makes it uniquely resistant to censorship and manipulation.

As we wrap up this exploration of blockchain technology, it's clear that its impact reaches far beyond cryptocurrency.

From finance to supply chain management, its applications are vast and varied.

Understanding blockchain is key to grasping the full potential of cryptocurrencies and the future of digital transactions.

As we continue, keep these foundational concepts in mind. They will serve as the building blocks for your cryptocurrency investing journey.

Getting Started with Crypto

Imagine entering a giant digital vault filled with countless opportunities, each representing a new way to shape the future of finance.

You don't walk around physically in this digital space like at a bank. Instead, you navigate with your fingertips—exploring the exciting opportunities of cryptocurrency right from your screen.

To participate, you need a **crypto wallet**, which is your personal vault for storing and managing digital assets.

It secures your cryptocurrencies and ensures you can send and receive them quickly.

But unlike a leather wallet that holds cash and cards, a crypto wallet manages **digital keys**. These keys unlock your funds on the blockchain.

Crypto wallets come in two forms: hot and cold.

Hot wallets are software-based, living on your computer or smartphone. They're always connected to the internet, offering convenience for frequent transactions.

This makes them ideal for day-to-day use. However, they're more susceptible to cyber threats because they're online.

On the other hand, **cold wallets** are hardware devices like USB sticks. They store your keys offline, providing robust security for long-term holdings.

They're less convenient for quick transactions but offer peace of mind against hacks. Picture them as a safe deposit box, secure but requiring a trip to access.

Choosing between custodial and non-custodial wallets is another decision on your journey.

Custodial wallets are akin to bank accounts. A third party holds your keys and manages security on your behalf.

This can be reassuring for beginners but means trusting someone else with your assets.

Non-custodial wallets, however, give you complete control. You hold the keys, making you solely responsible for their safety.

It's empowering but requires diligence in protecting your information. The choice depends on your comfort with managing digital security and your desire for control.

Throughout this book, I will cover several different wallets, exchanges, and other resources. I've created a Resources Page on my website with links to everything I mention here.

You can visit ArthurBellBooks.com/crypto.html or scan the QR code below to access the Resources Page.

Or visit
ArthurBellBooks.com/crypto.html
for **Helpful Resources** Related to
this book!

Before setting up your first wallet, I recommend creating a separate email account with a secure provider like **ProtonMail** to use exclusively for your crypto wallets and exchanges.

ProtonMail is free to use and offers several important advantages over regular email providers like Gmail or Yahoo:

Why Use ProtonMail?

- **Strong Security with End-to-End Encryption**
    - ProtonMail ensures that only you and the recipient can read your emails. Even ProtonMail itself can't

access your messages.

- Regular email providers don't typically offer this level of encryption.

- **Enhanced Privacy**

  - Based in Switzerland, ProtonMail benefits from strong privacy laws, which protect your data from government surveillance or requests.

  - In contrast, many regular email providers store data in jurisdictions with weaker privacy protections.

- **No Data Tracking**

  - ProtonMail doesn't log your IP address or track your activities, offering greater anonymity.

  - Regular email services often collect data for advertising and analytics.

- **Ad-Free and Open Source**

  - ProtonMail doesn't scan your emails to serve ads, and its open-source code ensures transparency and trust.

- **Protection Against Hacks**

  - With advanced security measures, ProtonMail reduces the risks of phishing and account breaches, making it ideal for sensitive crypto-related communications.

- **Self-Destructing Emails**

  - ProtonMail allows you to send emails that automatically expire after a set time, protecting sensitive information.

Pro Tip: Boost Your Security and Anonymity

When creating your ProtonMail account, use a password generator to create a strong and unique email address and password.

You can Google "strong password generator" to find several free ones.

Instead of using something easy to guess, like "johnsmith@ protonmail.com," you could generate something like "2!gq p4&23i@protonmail.com."

Use the same generator to create a secure password, write down this information, and store it in a private, safe location.

This extra step adds another layer of protection and anonymity, making it much harder for hackers to target your accounts.

Why This Matters

Using a secure email like ProtonMail and taking these extra precautions will significantly reduce the chances of compromised accounts, ensuring your crypto transactions remain private and protected.

Now, let's walk through setting up your first wallet.

In this chapter, we will focus on hot wallets and discuss cold wallets in greater detail later in the book.

When selecting a cryptocurrency wallet, choosing reputable options prioritizing security, user experience, and support for a wide range of digital assets is essential.

Here are some of the most reputable crypto wallets as of December 2024 - you can find all of these by doing a simple Google search:

- **Coinbase Wallet** is a user-friendly mobile wallet from the reputable Coinbase exchange. It supports numerous cryptocurrencies and provides seamless integration with the Coinbase platform.

- **Trust Wallet** is Binance's official mobile wallet. It supports a wide range of cryptocurrencies across multiple blockchains, offers a user-friendly mobile interface, and integrates with various decentralized applications.

- **Exodus Wallet** is a software wallet ideal for beginners. It offers an intuitive interface and support for multiple cryptocurrencies. The app also includes a built-in exchange feature, allowing for seamless trading within the app.

- **MetaMask** is a widely used browser extension and mobile wallet tailored for Ethereum and ERC-20 tokens. It facilitates easy interaction with decentralized applications (dApps) and the decentralized finance (DeFi) ecosystem.

- **ZenGo** is a mobile wallet that emphasizes security with keyless technology. It is user-friendly for both beginners and experienced users. It supports a variety of cryptocurrencies and offers features like savings and trading.

We'll be discussing exchanges momentarily (an exchange is a platform where you can buy, sell, and trade cryptocurrency).

After purchasing crypto on an exchange, you can transfer it to your wallet if you want to store it securely or use it elsewhere.

Coinbase and **Binance** are among the top exchanges, and starting with one of their wallets is the easiest way to get started.

Once you choose the wallet that you like best, download the app or software and follow the setup instructions.

When setting up your wallet, you'll create a strong password and generate a **backup phrase** (often called a **recovery** or **seed phrase**).

This phrase is your lifeline—it allows you to recover your wallet if you lose access to it.

Write the phrase down on paper and store it in a secure location, away from prying eyes, potential theft, and disasters like fire or water damage.

Remember, if you lose your backup phrase, you will lose access to your wallet and all the cryptocurrency stored in it.

There's no way to recover it without this phrase.

Next, strengthen your security by enabling two-factor authentication (2FA).

This adds an extra layer of protection by requiring a second form of verification to access your wallet.

For maximum security, use an authenticator app like **Authy** or **Google Authenticator** instead of relying on text messages or email, which can be more vulnerable to hacking.

These authenticator apps are free, easy to set up, and can be downloaded directly to your phone.

They generate time-sensitive codes that provide a secure and reliable way to protect your wallet.

Protecting Yourself in the Crypto World

Security is paramount in the world of cryptocurrency.

Regularly updating your wallet software is essential to patch vulnerabilities and guard against emerging threats.

Equally important is staying vigilant against phishing scams and malware, among the most common tactics hackers use to steal your credentials.

Understanding and Avoiding Phishing Scams

Phishing scams are fraudulent attempts to trick you into sharing sensitive information, such as your wallet credentials or backup phrase. These scams can take several forms, including:

- **Fake Emails**

    - Scammers may send emails that look like they're from a trusted exchange or wallet provider, asking you to "verify your account" or "resolve an issue."

    - These emails often include links to fake websites that steal your login details.

    - **What Not to Do:**

        - Never click on links in unsolicited emails.

        - Always type the official website address directly

into your browser.

- Verify the sender's email address—it should match the official domain of the exchange or wallet provider.

- **Malicious Links via Text or Messaging Apps**

  - You might receive text messages or messages on apps like WhatsApp or Telegram claiming to be from your exchange, asking you to log in via a provided link.

  - **What Not to Do:**

    - Legitimate exchanges will never send login links via text or messaging apps.

    - Avoid clicking on any links you receive through these channels.

- **Fake Websites**

  - Hackers create websites that look identical to real exchanges or wallet services to trick you into entering your credentials.

  - **What Not to Do:**

    - Double-check the website URL before logging in—look for slight misspellings or unusual domain extensions.

- Ensure the website uses HTTPS (look for a padlock icon in the browser's address bar).

- **Imposter Support Teams**

  - Scammers may pose as customer support representatives on social media or forums, offering to "help" with wallet or exchange issues.

  - **What Not to Do:**

    - Never share your backup phrase or private keys with anyone, even if they claim to be "support."

    - Always contact official support directly through verified channels.

Backup Phrase Safety

Keep your backup phrase offline and in a secure location, as it is the only way to recover your wallet if something goes wrong. Consider these options:

Store your backup phrase in a safe or a safety deposit box.

Avoid storing it digitally (e.g., in email, cloud storage, or a photo on your phone), as these methods are vulnerable to hacking.

Key Reminder

In the decentralized cryptocurrency world, no customer service can retrieve lost keys or recover hacked accounts. Your security is your responsibility, so take every precaution to safeguard your assets.

Wallet Security Checklist

- Select a reputable wallet provider.

- Create a strong, unique password.

- Generate and securely store your backup phrase.

- Enable two-factor authentication.

- Regularly update your wallet software.

- Be cautious of phishing emails and suspicious links.

Your wallet is more than just a digital storage space. It's the gateway to your crypto experience.

With it, you can explore the possibilities of digital currencies and be secure in knowing that your assets are protected.

As with any new venture, it requires learning and vigilance. But with these tools, you're ready to step confidently into cryptocurrency.

Choosing the Right Exchange: US vs International Options

There is a bustling digital marketplace where cryptocurrencies are bought and sold at the click of a button.

Cryptocurrency exchanges are the platforms that facilitate your entry into this digital marketplace.

Exchanges act like stock markets for digital assets, providing a space where you can trade your dollars for Bitcoin, Ethereum, or other cryptocurrencies.

There are two main types of exchanges: centralized and decentralized.

Centralized exchanges are like traditional banks, offering user-friendly interfaces and customer support but requiring you to trust them with your funds.

Decentralized exchanges, on the other hand, let you trade directly with others, keeping control of your assets in your hands.

The choice between these styles depends on your comfort level with technology and trust in third-party institutions.

Liquidity and trading volume are crucial when choosing an exchange.

Liquidity refers to how easily you can buy or sell an asset without affecting its price.

High liquidity means you can trade quickly and at competitive prices, so popular exchanges with many users are often preferred.

Trading volume, on the other hand, indicates the level of activity on the platform.

A high trading volume generally means better prices and faster transactions, as more buyers and sellers are available.

When choosing the best exchange for you, there are several standout options in the US and internationally.

Coinbase is a popular choice for those in the United States, especially for beginners.

Its user-friendly interface and strong security features make it an attractive option for those new to crypto.

Globally, **Binance** stands out as a leader, offering a wide range of cryptocurrencies and advanced trading options for more experienced users (Binance.com is for those outside of the United States, and Binance.us is for those within the US).

Kraken is another excellent US option if you want something tailored to advanced trading strategies.

Known for its robust security and comprehensive range of trading tools, it's ideal for those who wish to delve deeper into the trading aspect of cryptocurrency.

When selecting an exchange, consider several factors to ensure it meets your needs.

The user interface should be intuitive and easy to navigate, allowing you to execute trades without confusion.

Security features are equally important; look for exchanges with two-factor authentication and a reputation for protecting user data.

The range of available cryptocurrencies can also be a deciding factor, especially if you're interested in trading lesser-known altcoins.

Additionally, pay close attention to fee structures. Some exchanges charge higher transaction fees, affecting your profits, especially if you plan on frequent trading.

I've provided a list of the most reputable exchanges on the Resources Page at ArthurBellBooks.com/crypto.html. If anything changes, I'll update that list so you can rest assured the information is current.

Setting up an account on an exchange involves a process known as **Know Your Customer (KYC)**.

This standard procedure requires you to verify your identity by providing personal information and documentation.

You'll typically need to submit a picture of the front and back of a government-issued ID, proof of address, and sometimes even a selfie to complete this verification.

While this might seem intrusive, it's a necessary step to comply with regulations and protect against fraud.

Understanding account limits and restrictions is also crucial. Some exchanges limit the amount you can trade or withdraw, affecting your strategy, especially if you plan to make large transactions.

The world of cryptocurrency exchanges might seem daunting at first, but with the proper guidance, it becomes manageable.

Choosing the right exchange is a critical step in your crypto journey, as it will be your gateway to buying and selling digital assets.

Whether you prioritize ease of use, security, or a wide selection of cryptocurrencies, there's an exchange out there that fits your needs.

As you explore these options, consider the factors that matter most to you and align with your investment goals.

With some research and patience, you'll find the right platform for you, setting the stage for your success in the exciting world of cryptocurrency trading.

Setting Up Your Account: A Detailed Walkthrough

So, you've decided on an exchange and are ready to dive into cryptocurrency. The first step is setting up your account, which is simple if you follow the steps carefully.

Start by registering with your email address and phone number—these will serve as your primary communication points with the exchange.

Use an email you check regularly (or if you are following my advice, use the ProtonMail email address you set up previously) and ensure it's linked to a secure, private account.

For additional safety, avoid using a work or shared email address.

Next, create a strong, unique password. Think of this as the lock on your digital vault—make it complex and difficult to guess.

Avoid using common phrases or easily accessible personal details like birthdays or names.

Consider using a password manager to make managing your passwords easier and more secure.

These tools can generate and securely store strong passwords, protecting them from hackers or prying eyes.

After registration, you'll need to verify your email or phone number. This usually involves clicking a link sent to your email or entering a code sent to your phone.

Verifying your contact information ensures the exchange can communicate with you and adds an extra layer of security. Once confirmed, you're officially part of the crypto world.

With your account set up, it's time to fund it. This step is crucial because, without funds, you can't trade.

The most common method is linking your bank account. This lets you transfer money directly and usually involves entering your bank details and verifying small deposits.

It's straightforward and generally secure, provided you're using a trusted exchange.

Alternatively, you can use a credit or debit card for quicker transactions. Many exchanges offer this option, though it might come with higher fees.

If you already own some cryptocurrency, you can transfer it from another wallet.

This process varies slightly depending on the currency. Generally, it involves sending your crypto to a unique address provided by the exchange.

Navigating the exchange platform might seem daunting at first, but it becomes second nature with some practice.

Familiarize yourself with the dashboard, which is your command center. Here, you can view account balances, track market movements, and access trading tools.

Take time to explore the features available.

Placing buy and sell orders is the heart of trading, and understanding this process is key.

When you're ready to buy, you'll enter the amount you wish to purchase and the price you're willing to pay.

For selling, it's the reverse. Some exchanges offer advanced order types, like limit orders, which execute trades only at a specific price point.

These can be useful for strategic planning and mitigating risks.

Setting up price alerts and notifications can be immensely helpful as well.

Most exchanges allow you to set alerts for when a cryptocurrency reaches a specific price.

This feature keeps you informed without constantly checking the market, letting you react quickly to favorable conditions or protect against sudden drops.

With your account set up and funded, you can fully engage with the cryptocurrency market.

How to Buy and Sell Cryptocurrency on an Exchange: A Step-by-Step Guide

Here is a more detailed look to help you start buying and selling cryptocurrency. While each exchange may look slightly different, the process is generally similar across platforms. Below, we'll break it down step by step and explain key concepts like market and limit orders to help you get started confidently.

Step 1: Funding Your Account

Before you can buy crypto, you need to deposit funds into your exchange account.

1. Navigate to the **"Deposit"** or **"Add Funds"** section.

2. Choose your preferred payment method, such as a bank transfer, credit/debit card, or even transferring existing crypto.

3. Follow the instructions to complete the deposit. Keep in mind that some payment methods may have higher fees or longer processing times.

Step 2: Understanding Order Types

Exchanges typically offer several ways to buy and sell cryptocurrency:

- **Market Order**:

  - Executes your trade immediately at the current market price.

  - It is best for beginners who want a quick and straightforward purchase.

  - Example: If Bitcoin is trading at $20,000, a market order will buy or sell at that price (or close to it).

- **Limit Order**:

  - It allows you to set a specific price at which you want to buy or sell. The trade only happens if the market reaches your desired price.

  - It helps get better deals but may not execute immediately.

  - Example: You set a limit order to buy Bitcoin at $19,500. The order will only be filled if the price drops to $19,500.

- **Stop-Loss Order**:

  - Automatically sells your crypto if the price falls below a certain level, protecting you from further losses.

  - Example: If Bitcoin is at $20,000, you set a stop-loss at $19,000 to minimize losses if the price drops.

Step 3: Buying Cryptocurrency

1. Go to your exchange's **"Trade"** or **"Buy Crypto"** section.

2. Select the cryptocurrency you want to buy (e.g., Bitcoin, Ethereum).

3. Choose your order type (market or limit).

   ○ For a **market order**, enter the amount you want to spend (e.g., $100) or the amount of crypto you want to buy (e.g., 0.005 BTC).

   ○ For a **limit order**, specify the price and amount you want to buy.

4. Review your order details and confirm the purchase.

Step 4: Selling Cryptocurrency

Selling crypto works similarly to buying:

1. Navigate to the **"Trade"** or **"Sell Crypto"** section.

2. Select the cryptocurrency you want to sell.

3. Choose your order type (market or limit).

   ○ For a **market order**, enter the amount of crypto you want to sell.

- For a **limit order**, specify the price and amount you want to sell.

4. Review your order and confirm the sale.

Step 5: Checking Your Portfolio

After buying or selling, you can check your portfolio to monitor your investments:

1. Go to the **"Portfolio"** or **"My Assets"** section of the exchange.

2. View your holdings, which typically show:

   - The amount of each cryptocurrency you own.

   - The current market value of each asset.

   - Your total portfolio value.

3. Many exchanges also provide graphs and tools to track changes in value over time.

Tips for Managing Your Crypto Investments

- **Monitor Prices Regularly**: Use the exchange's price charts to stay updated on market movements.

- **Understand Fees**: Be aware of trading fees, withdrawal fees, and other applicable costs.

- **Use Security Features**: Enable two-factor authentication (2FA) and use a secure email for your account.

- **Withdraw to a Wallet**: Consider transferring your purchased crypto to a personal wallet for added security.

Following these steps, you can confidently buy, sell, and track your cryptocurrency investments. As you gain experience, you can explore more advanced features offered by exchanges to refine your strategy.

The steps you've taken are more than just procedural. They lay the groundwork for your future in crypto, giving you the tools and knowledge to trade confidently.

As we wrap up this chapter, remember that setting up your account is just the beginning. It's your entry point into an exciting and dynamic world.

Next, we'll explore strategies for navigating the market and making informed investment decisions.

Navigating the Crypto Market

A single number can tell you so much about a cryptocurrency. That's the magic of **market capitalization**, often called **"market cap."**

It's a key metric savvy investors use to gauge the size and health of a cryptocurrency.

Imagine you're looking at a map of a city, where each building represents a cryptocurrency.

Some buildings are towering skyscrapers, symbolizing well-established, widely-used cryptocurrencies like Bitcoin or Ethereum.

Others are small shops, representing newer or less popular coins.

Market cap is like the height of each building—it shows how "big" or established a cryptocurrency is in terms of its overall value.

Market cap is calculated by multiplying the price of a single coin by the total number of coins in circulation.

This simple formula provides a quick snapshot of a cryptocurrency's size and liquidity, helping you gauge its potential stability and popularity when making investment decisions.

Understanding Market Cap: The Building Blocks of Crypto

Market cap is a key measure of a cryptocurrency's size and market presence.

Think of large-cap cryptocurrencies, with a market cap of over $10 billion, as the towering skyscrapers in the city.

They're well-established, stable, and often shape the entire market. Examples include giants like Bitcoin and Ethereum.

Mid-cap cryptocurrencies, with market caps between $1 billion and $10 billion, are like growing businesses with strong potential. They're more stable than smaller coins but still have room to expand.

Small-cap cryptocurrencies, with market caps under $1 billion, are like boutique shops—exciting and full of potential but more unpredictable. They can grow quickly but are also more likely to face setbacks.

Knowing whether a coin is a skyscraper, a growing business, or a boutique shop can help you weigh its risks and rewards when investing.

How Market Cap Affects Price and Liquidity

Market cap and price movements are closely connected.

When optimism is high in bull markets, skyscraper coins (large caps) often grow steadily as investors trust their stability.

On the other hand, boutique coins (small caps) can see wild price swings during bear markets when uncertainty is high.

Trading volume plays a role, too. Coins with a high market cap often have high trading volume, meaning many people buy and sell them.

This makes the market liquid, so you can buy or sell quickly without causing significant price changes.

Liquidity is crucial for investors who want to move in or out of positions easily while keeping their investments safe.

Using Market Cap to Make Smarter Investments

Market cap is a powerful tool for analyzing cryptocurrencies.

A great, free resource for checking the market cap is CoinGecko.com.

This website lists cryptocurrencies from largest to smallest market cap, making it easy to see how different coins stack up.

Coins with a higher market cap, such as Bitcoin or Ethereum, are often more stable and less volatile. These "skyscrapers" are ideal for conservative investors prioritizing steady growth and lower risk.

On the other hand, coins with a smaller market cap carry more risk. Still, they may offer more significant potential for high returns—these "boutique shops" are better suited for more adventurous investors looking for rapid growth opportunities.

Exercise: Analyze Market Cap Using CoinGecko

1. **Visit CoinGecko.com**

- Explore the list of cryptocurrencies and focus on the "Market Cap" column.

2. **Choose Three Cryptocurrencies**

- Select three coins that interest you. Pick a mix of large-cap, mid-cap, and small-cap coins for variety.

3. **Analyze the Data**

- Write down each coin's market cap, then click on each coin to see the coin's chart and more information about the coin.

- Look at recent changes in market cap—has it grown or declined?

- Consider how this aligns with your investment goals. For example:

  - Are you looking for stability? Focus on large-cap coins.

  - Willing to take more risk for potentially higher returns? Look at mid- or small-cap coins.

4. **Reflect on Your Portfolio**

- Consider how these coins might fit into your investment strategy based on your findings.

- Ask yourself: Does this mix of coins match my risk tolerance and financial objectives?

Looking Beyond Market Cap: Building a Complete Investment Strategy

While market cap is a valuable tool, it's only one part of the bigger picture.

To make informed investment decisions, you'll also want to evaluate the following key factors, many of which you can find on CoinGecko.com:

1. **Coin's Fundamentals**

   - This refers to the basics of the cryptocurrency, including its purpose, mission, and technology.

   - On CoinGecko, check the coin's description and technical documentation (like a whitepaper) to understand its goals and how it works.

2. **The Team Behind the Coin**

   - A strong team of developers and leaders increases confidence in the coin's potential.

   - Look for profiles or links to team members on CoinGecko or the coin's official website. Are they experienced? Do they have a track record of success?

3. **Use Case**

   - The use case is the problem the cryptocurrency

aims to solve or the value it brings to users.

- For example, Bitcoin is a decentralized store of value, while Ethereum powers smart contracts and decentralized apps. The coin's use case is listed on CoinGecko under its project description.

4. **Overall Market Trends**

- This involves looking at the bigger picture of the crypto market. Are most coins trending upward or downward? Is there significant news influencing prices?

- On CoinGecko, you can view charts showing market trends and recent news updates that may impact the crypto space.

How to Use This Information

- Start by exploring CoinGecko to learn about the coins you're interested in.

- To assess its potential, combine what you discover about the coin's fundamentals, team, and use case with its market cap.

- Pay attention to overall market trends to decide whether the current environment is favorable for investing.

You can create a more well-rounded investment strategy by considering all these factors together.

Remember, no single metric tells the whole story—market cap, fundamentals, and trends all play a role in making wise investment decisions.

Safest Coins to Invest In: Minimizing Risk

As you learn more about cryptocurrency investing, it's common to consider which coins provide more stability in the highly volatile crypto market.

While no investment is without risk, some cryptocurrencies are generally considered more stable and trustworthy thanks to specific characteristics.

One key trait is an established history. Coins that have been around for several years have weathered market ups and downs, proving their resilience.

They often boast a strong community of supporters who believe in the coin's mission and use case, providing a foundation of trust and continuity.

This communal backing bolsters the coin's credibility and helps stabilize its value.

Another important factor is high liquidity, which ensures you can buy or sell without causing wild price swings.

Liquidity is often linked to high market capitalization, suggesting a large number of active participants in the trading of the coin.

When a coin has both a robust market cap and liquidity, it's more likely to withstand sudden market changes.

This makes it a more reliable choice for those new to crypto or those looking to minimize risk.

Additionally, the development team behind the coin plays a vital role. A transparent team with a clear roadmap inspires confidence, showing their commitment to the project's long-term success.

When considering specific coins, Bitcoin (BTC) naturally comes to mind.

As the first and most well-known cryptocurrency, Bitcoin has paved the way for digital currencies.

It's often referred to as **digital gold** due to its standing in the market.

Its extensive network and widespread acceptance make it a cornerstone of many investment portfolios.

Then there's Ethereum (ETH), known for its robust network that supports decentralized applications and smart contracts.

Ethereum's ongoing developments, like the Ethereum 2.0 upgrade, strengthen its position in the market.

Lastly, stablecoins such as USDC provide an interesting option for those looking to hedge against volatility.

Pegged to traditional currencies like the US dollar, they offer stability while allowing you to remain within the crypto ecosystem.

Diversification is a strategy that can help mitigate risk.

Just as you wouldn't put all your eggs in one basket, spreading your investments across different cryptocurrencies can safeguard against market volatility.

Balancing between large-cap coins that offer stability and small-cap coins that have higher growth potential is key.

Including stablecoins in your portfolio can buffer against sudden market downturns.

This mix of assets can help smooth out the fluctuations that are all too common with cryptocurrency.

Conducting due diligence before investing is a must. This means doing your homework and researching the coins you're interested in.

Start by evaluating the development team. Are they transparent? Do they have a track record of success in the crypto space?

A solid team with a clear vision is often a good sign. Look at the project roadmap to see if they're meeting their goals and progressing.

Also, the historical performance of the coin should be considered.

While past performance doesn't guarantee future results, it can provide insights into how the coin responds to market changes.

Lastly, gauge market sentiment. Are people confident in the coin's future, or are there concerns that could affect its value?

Being informed and prepared is your best defense against unnecessary risk.

As you explore the world of cryptocurrency, keep these principles in mind. You can confidently navigate the crypto market with careful planning and thoughtful decision-making.

The BTC Rainbow Chart: Understanding and Utilizing It

The BTC Rainbow Chart is an easy and visual way to understand Bitcoin's price trends.

You can see this chart in real-time at https://www.blockchaincenter.net/en/bitcoin-rainbow-chart/.

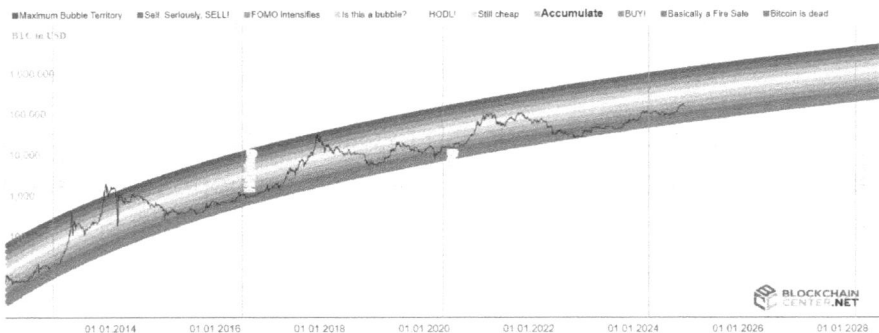

This simple yet powerful tool uses color-coded bands to represent market sentiment.

Each band on the chart provides insight into Bitcoin's valuation, from deep blues and purples indicating potential undervaluation to fiery reds signaling possible overvaluation.

Consider it a roadmap that helps you evaluate whether it might be a good time to buy, hold, or sell—making complex price data easier to interpret.

The BTC Rainbow Chart is built upon historical price data, plotted over time, to give investors a sense of long-term trends versus short-term fluctuations.

It's like having a weather map for Bitcoin, showing you the climate of the market at a glance.

But how do you interpret these colorful bands? Let's break it down.

The lower bands, often in cooler hues like blue and indigo, suggest that Bitcoin is undervalued, potentially offering a "buy" signal.

As we move up the spectrum to warmer colors—yellows and oranges—the chart indicates a more neutral or "hold" sentiment.

Finally, the upper bands, awash in reds and pinks, warn of possible overvaluation, hinting that it might be time to consider selling.

However, it's important to approach the BTC Rainbow Chart with a balanced perspective.

While it provides a visually engaging overview of Bitcoin's historical price behavior, it's not a crystal ball.

It lacks predictive power for future prices, relying on past data to identify trends.

While it can suggest potential opportunities, it should never be your sole guide in making investment decisions.

Think of it as a piece of the puzzle that should be combined with other analytical tools and personal research.

You can develop a more comprehensive strategy by integrating the Rainbow Chart with fundamental analysis, market news, and other technical indicators.

Consider some historical instances where the BTC Rainbow Chart has been particularly insightful.

During past bull markets, the chart's color bands gradually shifted from cool to warm, reflecting the growing optimism and increased buying pressure.

Savvy investors who paid attention to these transitions were able to ride the wave, capturing significant gains.

Conversely, when the chart's colors deepened into reds, it signaled caution, prompting many to reassess their positions.

You can tailor your strategy to fit your risk tolerance and financial objectives by aligning these visual cues with your personal investment goals.

What the Colors Indicate

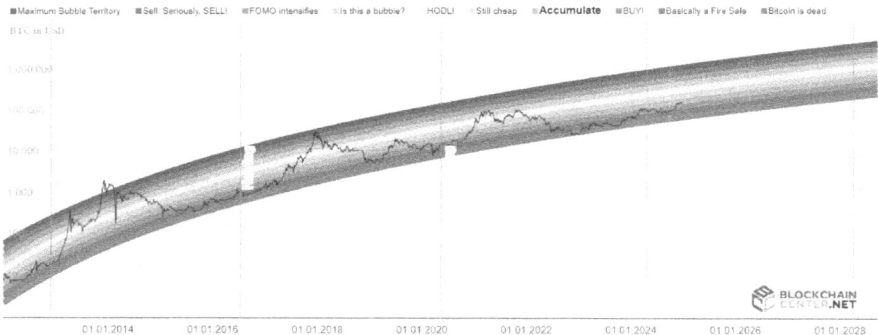

- **Lower Bands (Blue/Purple):** Considered undervalued, potentially a buying opportunity.

- **Middle Bands (Yellow/Orange):** Neutral valuation, suggesting a hold strategy.

- **Upper Bands (Red/Pink):** Seen as overvalued, indicating a possible sell zone.

To effectively use the BTC Rainbow Chart, it's essential to remember its limitations.

It's a lagging indicator, meaning it's more reliable for understanding past trends rather than predicting immediate future movements.

The chart doesn't account for external factors like macroeconomic changes or sudden market events, which can greatly influence Bitcoin's price.

It serves best as a component of a broader investment strategy, providing a historical context that can inform but not dictate your decisions.

The BTC Rainbow Chart is a vibrant tool that offers a unique perspective on Bitcoin's price dynamics.

While it's not infallible, it can be a valuable part of your investment toolkit, offering visually appealing and informative insights.

As you continue to explore the crypto market, consider how the Rainbow Chart might complement your broader strategy, providing a colorful lens through which to view Bitcoin's journey.

Next, we'll dive into investment strategies and techniques, exploring how to apply these insights practically.

Investment Strategies and Techniques

Investing in cryptocurrency offers multiple approaches, each with its opportunities and challenges.

The two main strategies to consider are **long-term** and **short-term investing**.

Choosing the right strategy depends on your goals, risk tolerance, and financial priorities.

Understanding these approaches is key to developing a plan that aligns with your needs and helps you navigate the dynamic world of crypto.

Long-term investing, often called the "buy and hold" strategy, is like planting a tree.

You dig a hole, place the sapling, and wait patiently, trusting it will grow tall and strong with time.

In crypto, holding onto your cryptocurrency for years is known as **HODLing**.

The term originated from a 2013 online forum post where a user misspelled "hold" during a market crash, and it quickly became a badge of honor for long-term investors who resist the urge to sell during volatility.

HODLing involves riding out the market's ups and downs, reducing exposure to the daily fluctuations that can be nerve-wracking.

Over time, this strategy offers the potential for significant appreciation. Many have seen impressive returns by simply holding onto their assets as the market matured.

However, the risk is that you might miss out on short-term gains, as opportunities to capitalize on sudden market spikes can slip by unnoticed.

Conversely, short-term trading is more like surfing. You watch the waves, timing your entry to ride them for as long as possible.

It's a dynamic, fast-paced approach where trades happen within days, weeks, or even hours.

The appeal is clear: the opportunity for quick profits. By capitalizing on short-term price movements, traders can potentially reap rewards rapidly.

However, this path is fraught with pitfalls. Transaction costs and taxes can quickly erode profits, and the constant exposure to market volatility demands a thick skin.

It's a strategy that requires time, attention, and expertise to execute successfully.

Navigating the volatile crypto market can be challenging, whether you're focused on short-term trades or long-term investments.

Fortunately, there's a powerful tool that can help streamline your strategy: **bot trading**.

Automated trading bots can execute trades based on pre-set rules, helping you take advantage of market opportunities without constant monitoring.

Later in this book, we'll dedicate an entire chapter to exploring bot trading, including how it works and how to set it up.

For now, take a moment to think about the trading approach that suits you best—whether it's the fast-paced world of short-term trading or the patience-driven strategy of long-term investing.

Understanding your preferences will help you decide how bot trading best complements your goals.

Deciding which path to take involves introspection.

Start by assessing your risk tolerance. Are you comfortable with the idea of holding your investments through market swings? Or are you drawn to the thrill of chasing quick profits?

Consider your financial goals as well. Are you investing for retirement, aiming to grow your wealth over decades? Or are you looking to generate income in the near term?

These questions will help clarify your direction.

Time commitment is another critical factor. Long-term investing requires minimal daily oversight, making it suitable for those with busy schedules or wanting to minimize stress.

In contrast, short-term trading demands regular monitoring and quick decision-making. It's a more active endeavor that can be rewarding for those who enjoy the challenge and have the time to dedicate to it.

Finally, evaluate your trading expertise. Long-term investing is relatively straightforward and requires less technical knowledge. It's accessible for beginners and those who prefer a more straightforward approach.

On the other hand, short-term trading benefits from a deeper understanding of market trends and technical analysis. It's a skill that can be developed over time but requires dedication and practice.

Finding Your Investment Path

Answer these questions honestly:

- **Reflect on your risk tolerance:** Are you comfortable with volatility or prefer stability?

- **Consider your financial goals:** Are you investing for long-term growth or short-term income?

- **Evaluate your time availability:** Can you commit to active trading or prefer a passive approach?

- **Assess your trading knowledge:** Are you confident in your ability to analyze market trends and make informed decisions?

Choosing the right investment path is a personal decision. You can navigate the crypto market more confidently and clearly by aligning your strategy with your lifestyle, goals, and risk appetite.

Remember, there's no one-size-fits-all approach. It's about finding the path that resonates with you and adjusting as you gain experience and your circumstances evolve.

Diversification: Spreading Your Investments Wisely

Think of your investment portfolio like a garden. If you plant only one type of flower, a single pest or disease could wipe it all out.

But by planting a variety, you protect your garden from total devastation.

This is the essence of diversification—spreading your investments across different assets to reduce risk and enhance stability.

In other words, don't put all your eggs in one basket.

By balancing risk, you mitigate the impact of poor-performing investments, ensuring that if one asset takes a hit, others can help cushion the blow.

This strategy is vital in a volatile market like cryptocurrency, where fortunes can change overnight.

Within the cryptocurrency market, there are several ways to diversify.

First, consider investing in a mix of cryptocurrencies.

Bitcoin might be the king of crypto, but altcoins offer unique opportunities. They can sometimes outperform Bitcoin during certain market conditions.

By including a variety of altcoins in your portfolio, you not only tap into different market segments but also stand a chance to benefit from their individual growth spurts.

Furthermore, utility tokens, which grant access to specific services within a blockchain ecosystem, and security tokens, which represent ownership of an asset, can add another layer of diversification.

Their distinct utility and regulatory framework offer different risk and reward profiles.

Allocating a portion of your portfolio to stablecoins is also wise. These are pegged to traditional currencies like the US dollar, providing stability amidst the market's ups and downs.

While they may not offer high returns, they help preserve your portfolio's value during turbulent times.

Here are some of the most popular stablecoins:

- **Tether (USDT)**

  - Launched in 2014, Tether is the most widely used stablecoin, pegged to the U.S. dollar. It facilitates trading without the volatility typical of other cryptocurrencies.

- **USD Coin (USDC)**

  - Introduced by Circle and Coinbase in 2018, USDC emphasizes transparency and regulatory compliance, with reserves audited monthly to ensure full backing by U.S. dollars.

- **Binance USD (BUSD)**

  - Issued by Binance in partnership with Paxos, BUSD is fully backed by U.S. dollars held in FDIC-insured accounts and short-term U.S. Treasury bills, offering fast transaction speeds and minimal fees within the Binance ecosystem.

- **Dai (DAI)**

  - A decentralized stablecoin governed by Maker-DAO, DAI is backed by a mix of cryptocurrencies, maintaining its peg to the U.S. dollar through an algorithmic system that adjusts collateral requirements.

- **TrueUSD (TUSD)**

  - Created by TrustToken, TUSD focuses on transparency and regulatory compliance, backed by U.S. dollar reserves held in third-party accounts and verified through daily attestations.

But diversification shouldn't end with cryptocurrencies. A well-rounded portfolio looks beyond digital assets to include traditional investments.

Stocks and bonds are the bedrock of many investment strategies. Stocks offer growth potential and dividends, while bonds provide steady, reliable income.

Real estate is another option, delivering tangible value and potential rental income. It's a great way to hedge against inflation and add a physical asset to your investments.

Commodities like gold and silver have long been considered safe havens in times of economic uncertainty. They provide a store of value that can protect your portfolio from financial turmoil.

Combining cryptocurrencies with these traditional assets creates a balanced portfolio that can weather various economic conditions.

Maintaining a diversified portfolio requires regular attention. It's not a set-and-forget strategy.

Start by setting clear diversification goals. Decide what percentage of your portfolio you want to allocate to each type of investment.

This will guide your decision-making and help you stay on track.

Regularly review and rebalance your portfolio to ensure it aligns with your goals. Markets change, and so should your portfolio.

If one asset class has grown significantly, it might be time to redistribute some profits to underperforming areas.

Stay informed about market developments. Changes in the economic landscape or emerging technologies can impact your investments, and being up-to-date allows you to make informed decisions.

Diversification is not just a strategy; it's a mindset. It requires you to think about the bigger picture and how each piece of your portfolio fits together.

By spreading your investments wisely, you protect yourself from unexpected downturns and position yourself for long-term success. You want to build a resilient portfolio that can thrive in any market environment.

Trading Strategies: Reading Charts and Market Trends

Imagine you're a detective, piecing together clues to solve a mystery. Trading in cryptocurrency is similar; it involves analyzing patterns and signals to predict future market movements.

This is where technical analysis comes in. It's a powerful tool that uses historical price data to forecast where prices might be heading.

By identifying trends and patterns, traders can make informed decisions like a detective following a trail of evidence.

The beauty of technical analysis lies in its ability to distill vast amounts of data into actionable insights.

At the heart of technical analysis are chart patterns and indicators.

I will show you some images of charts, which can be accessed on CoinGecko. On the homepage, you would click on the cryptocurrency you'd like to investigate further, then, where you see the chart, choose **Trading View**.

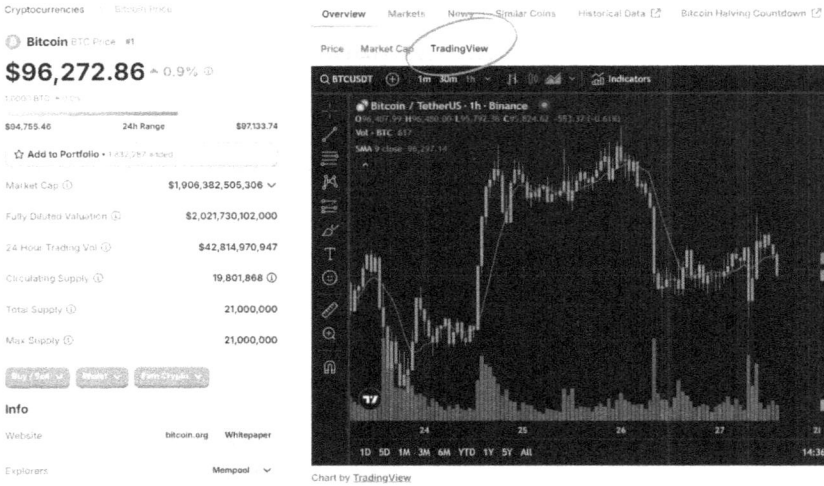

Moving Averages

A **moving average** is a simple tool for smoothing out a cryptocurrency's price changes so you can more easily see trends.

To access the chart's moving averages, click **Indicators** and scroll through the options until you find the **Moving Averages** options.

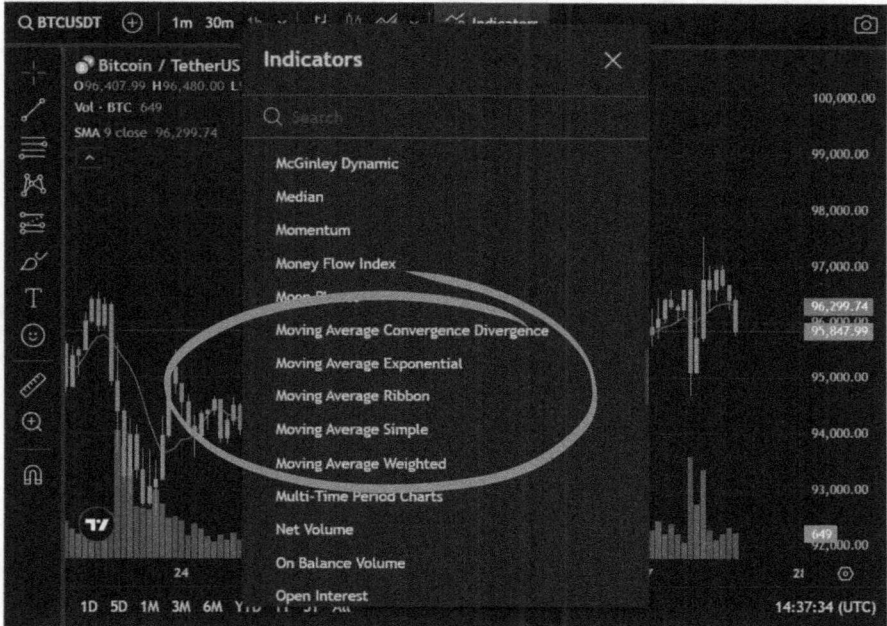

You can play with each of them to see which one you like best, but the example I'm showing you here is the **"Moving Average Simple"** option.

If you look at this Bitcoin price chart, where the price jumps up and down daily, it can be hard to spot patterns. A moving average adds a smooth line that shows the average price over a specific period.

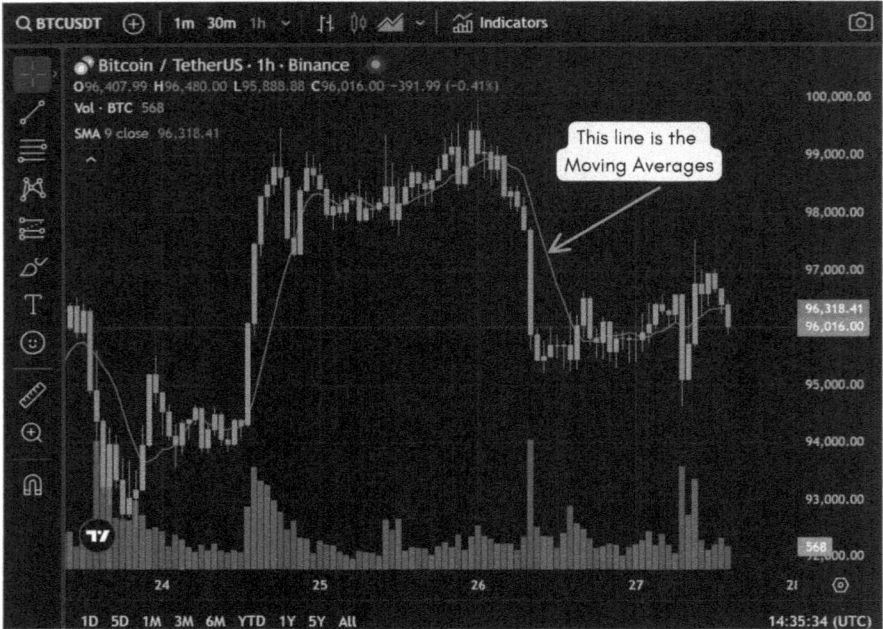

For example:

- A **short-term moving average**, like the **10-day average**, follows the price closely and shows recent trends.

- A **long-term moving average**, like the **200-day average**, moves more slowly and shows the bigger picture over time.

On a chart, you might notice moments when the short-term moving average crosses above the long-term moving average. This is called a **golden cross** and is often seen as a sign that prices may keep rising.

When the short-term average crosses below the long-term average, it's called a **death cross** and might suggest prices could fall.

Traders use these lines to help decide when to buy or sell, making it easier to spot market trends.

Relative Strength Index (RSI)

The **Relative Strength Index (RSI)**, another popular indicator, measures the speed and change of price movements, alerting you to overbought or oversold conditions.

To access the chart's RSI, click **Indicators** and scroll through the options until you find the **Connors RSI** option.

The **Relative Strength Index (RSI)** is like a thermometer for the market. It tells you whether a cryptocurrency might be too "hot" (overbought) or too "cold" (oversold) by looking at how fast and how much its price has been changing.

Here's how it works:

1. **What RSI Measures**:

   ◦ RSI looks at the recent price changes of a cryptocurrency and gives you a number between **0 and 100**.

   ◦ This number shows whether the price has been rising or falling too quickly.

2. **Key Levels to Know**:

- **Above 70**: The cryptocurrency might be over-bought when the RSI is over 70. This means many people have been buying, and the price could be too high for its value. It's often a signal that the price might drop soon.

- **Below 30**: The cryptocurrency might be oversold when the RSI is under 30. This means many people have been selling, and the price could be too low. It's often a signal that the price might rise soon.

3. **Why It's Useful**:

- RSI helps traders decide if they should buy or sell. For example:

  - If Bitcoin's RSI is at 80, it might mean the price is too high, and you should wait for it to drop before buying.

  - If Bitcoin's RSI is at 20, it might mean the price is too low, and it could be a good time to buy.

4. **How It's Shown on a Chart**:

- The RSI is usually shown as a separate line below a price chart. The line moves up and down between 0 and 100, making it easy to see when the price might be overbought or oversold.

Imagine Bitcoin's price has been rising quickly for several days. The RSI might climb to 75, suggesting it's overbought. A smart trader might decide to wait instead of buying, expecting the price to drop soon.

On the flip side, if Bitcoin's price has been falling for days and the RSI drops to 25, the market might have overreacted, and the price could bounce back. This could be a signal to buy.

The RSI gives you a quick way to judge the market's mood and avoid emotional decisions.

While imperfect, it's a helpful tool when combined with other indicators like moving averages or market trends.

Support and Resistance Levels

There are also **support** and **resistance levels**—imaginary lines prices often struggle to break through. Understanding these levels can help you anticipate potential reversals or breakouts.

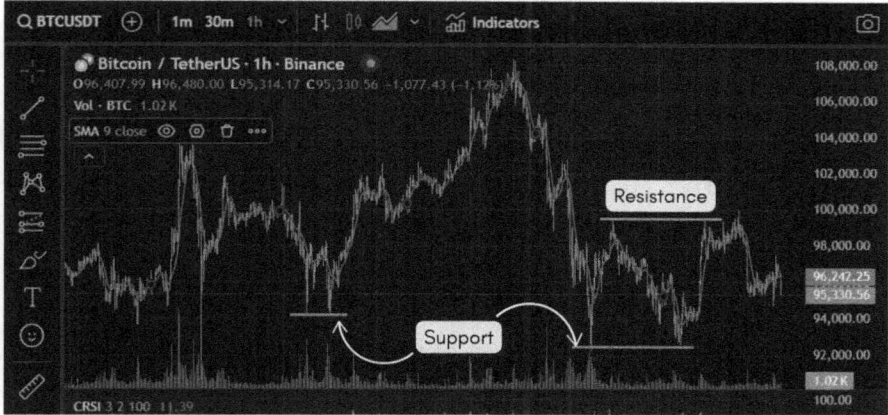

Bitcoin / TetherUS · 1h · Binance
O96,407.99 H96,480.00 L95,314.17 C95,330.56 -1,077.43 (-1.12%)
Vol · BTC 1.02K
SMA 9 close

Resistance

Support

108,000.00
106,000.00
104,000.00
102,000.00
100,000.00
98,000.00
96,242.25
95,330.56
94,000.00
92,000.00
1.02K
100.00

With their unique formations, **Candlestick patterns also** tell a story about market sentiment. They can reveal whether buyers or sellers are in control, providing critical clues for your trading strategy.

Think of support and resistance as invisible barriers that prices tend to bounce off of:

1. **Support Levels**:

   - A **support level** is like a floor for the price. It's a point where a cryptocurrency's price stops falling and starts going back up.

   - Why does this happen? At this level, buyers step in because they see the price as a good deal. This demand prevents the price from dropping further.

   - Example: If Bitcoin keeps bouncing back up whenever it hits $20,000, then $20,000 is a support level.

2. **Resistance Levels**:

- A **resistance level** is like a ceiling for the price. It's a point where the price stops rising and starts going down.

- Why? At this level, sellers jump in because they think the price is too high and want to cash out. This supply prevents the price from going higher.

- Example: If Bitcoin struggles to go above $25,000, then $25,000 is a resistance level.

Understanding these levels helps you predict when a price might **reverse** (bounce back) or **break out** (move beyond the barrier).

If a price breaks through resistance, it might keep rising, and if it falls below support, it might keep dropping.

Candlestick Patterns

Candlesticks are a type of chart used to track price movements over a specific period, like an hour, a day, or a week.

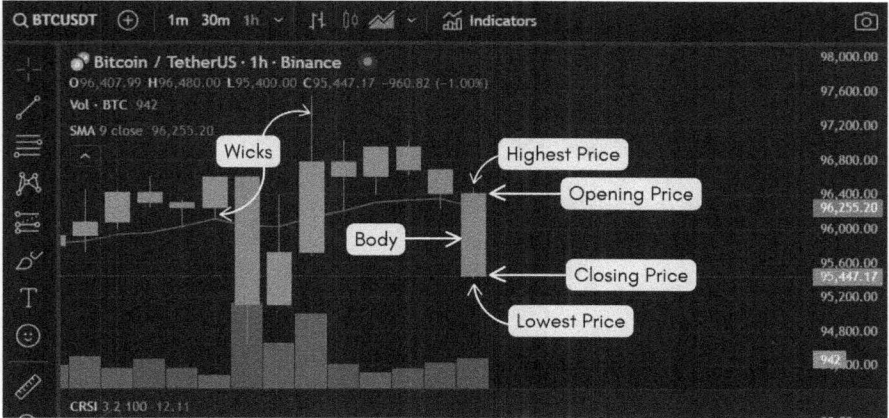

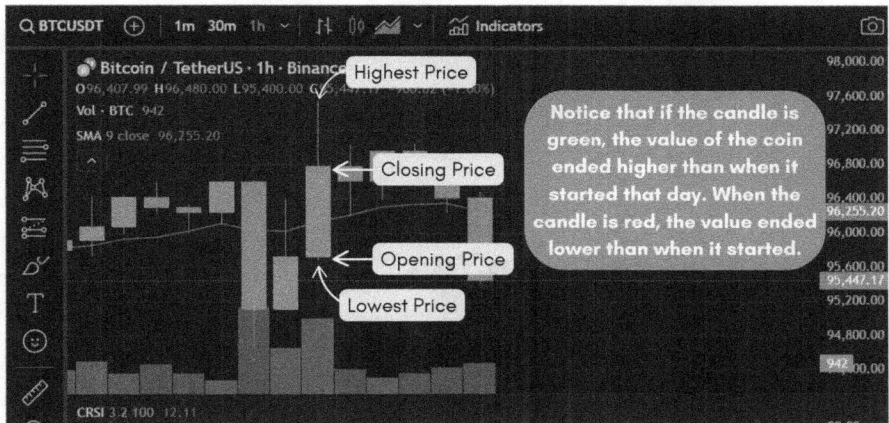

Each candlestick shows four key pieces of information:

1. The **opening price** (where the price started at the beginning of the time period).

2. The **closing price** (where the price ended at the end of the time period).

3. The **highest price** reached during that period.

4. The **lowest price** reached during that period.

The candlestick looks like a box with lines (called "wicks") sticking out of the top and bottom:

- The **box** is called the **body**.

  - If the price closed higher than it opened, the body is usually green (or white)—this means buyers were in control.

  - If the price closes lower than it opened, the body will be red (or black)—this means sellers are in control.

- The **wicks** show the high and low prices during that period.

How These Tools Help You

- **Support and Resistance**:

  - Use these levels to decide when to buy or sell. For example, buy near support (when the price is low) and sell near resistance (when the price is high).

- **Candlestick Patterns**:

  - By analyzing candlesticks, you can understand whether buyers or sellers are in charge and predict what might happen next. For example:

- A small body with long wicks (called a **"doji"**) means the market is indecisive.

- A strong green candlestick with no wicks suggests buyers are entirely in control.

Let's say Bitcoin has been trading at $20,000, which has been its support level for weeks. You notice on a candlestick chart that a strong green candlestick has formed near $20,000. This could signal that the price is about to bounce back up, and you might decide to buy.

Understanding support, resistance, and candlestick patterns gives you the tools to anticipate price movements and make smarter trading decisions.

Trading strategies, much like chess openings, come with their own set of rules and potential outcomes.

Day trading is for those who thrive on adrenaline and quick decisions. It involves buying and selling within the same day, aiming to profit from small price movements.

The fast pace means it's not for everyone, as it requires constant monitoring and a keen eye for detail.

Swing trading, however, captures gains from price swings over days or weeks. It's less frantic than day trading but still demands attention and strategy.

Scalping focuses on exploiting small price gaps for numerous quick profits. It's akin to a hummingbird sipping nectar—a rapid, precise approach that requires discipline and a knack for timing.

Creating a personalized trading plan is like drafting a roadmap for your financial goals.

Start by setting clear entry and exit points for each trade. Knowing when to enter or leave a position helps avoid emotional decisions driven by fear or greed.

Establishing stop-loss limits is crucial, too. These are predetermined points at which you'll exit a losing trade to prevent further losses, acting as a safety net for your investments.

Regularly evaluate your performance, analyzing what worked and what didn't. This reflection allows you to adjust your strategies, improve over time, and learn from both successes and failures.

In the broader context of crypto investing, having a solid trading strategy is like having a well-oiled machine. It ensures that your moves are deliberate and informed rather than reactionary.

As you integrate these strategies into your approach, remember that they are tools—meant to enhance your understanding and execution in the market.

Each strategy offers a unique lens to view market dynamics, providing insights that can guide your actions.

Mastering these techniques is a continuous process that requires patience, practice, and a commitment to learning.

As you grow more comfortable with technical analysis and trading strategies, you'll make decisions more confidently and precisely.

Next, we'll explore how to protect your investments and manage risks, ensuring your crypto journey remains secure and prosperous.

Security and Risk Management

Your cryptocurrency holdings are like a treasure chest. This chest holds not just your wealth but the dreams you've attached to it—your child's education, a dream home, or a comfortable retirement.

But without the proper security measures, this chest is vulnerable to digital pirates lurking in the vast sea of the internet.

Protecting your crypto assets is paramount, and it all starts with understanding the critical role of private keys and seed phrases.

These are your keys to the kingdom, granting access to your digital assets. Lose them, and you could be locked out of your wealth forever.

Private keys are unique strings of characters that authorize the transactions of your cryptocurrencies.

Think of them as the secret code that allows you to manage your funds.

But private keys are irreplaceable, unlike passwords you can reset and change often. This is why safeguarding them is essential.

Alongside private keys, **seed phrases** are equally important.

A seed phrase is a series of words generated by your wallet. It acts as a backup, allowing you to recover your wallet and assets if you ever lose access.

The best way to protect these is by storing them offline, away from the reach of hackers.

Write your seed phrase down on paper and store it in a safe place, such as a locked drawer or a safety deposit box.

Never keep digital copies, as these can be easily compromised.

Password Managers

With the growing sophistication of cyber threats, using a **password manager** securely can enhance your defenses.

These tools store and manage your passwords, ensuring they are strong and unique.

A password manager can generate complex passwords for your accounts, reducing the risk of unauthorized access.

However, choose a reputable manager and protect it with a strong master password that only you know.

ProtonMail offers a great password manager, but I'll provide you with a more detailed list on the Resources Page at ArthurBellBooks.com/crypto.html.

Multifactor Authentication (MFA)

Multifactor authentication (MFA) adds another layer of protection around your crypto accounts. It's like having a double lock on your front door.

MFA requires you to provide two or more verification factors to gain access to your account.

As discussed in a previous chapter, when you set up your first exchange account, you can use apps like Authy or Google Authenticator.

They generate time-sensitive codes that you enter alongside your password. This extra step may seem cumbersome, but it significantly enhances security by requiring physical access to a second device.

Hardware Wallets (Cold Wallets)

A **cold wallet** (or **hardware wallet**) is a storage solution for your offline digital assets, safeguarding them from hackers who roam the internet.

Because it doesn't connect to the web, it's considered one of the most secure cryptocurrency storage methods.

This offline nature makes cold wallets particularly suitable for long-term holding, providing peace of mind for those who plan to store their assets for extended periods without frequent transactions.

Hardware wallets like **Ledger Nano S** and **Trezor** are popular choices among the various types of cold wallets.

These devices resemble USB sticks and can be plugged into your computer when you need to access your funds. They store your private keys offline, ensuring your assets are safe from online threats.

Paper wallets present another cost-effective option. These are simply pieces of paper with your private and public keys printed on them.

While they're immune to digital attacks, they require careful handling to avoid physical damage or loss.

Then, there are **metal wallets**, which are essentially indestructible. Made of materials like stainless steel or titanium, they provide durability and protection against fire or water damage, offering an extra layer of security for your printed keys.

Setting up a cold wallet might seem daunting, but it's straightforward with some guidance.

Start with purchasing a hardware wallet from a trusted re-tailer. Once you have your device, follow the manufacturer's instructions to install the necessary software on your computer.

During the initial setup, you'll create a backup seed phrase—a series of words that act as a recovery tool if your wallet is lost or damaged.

Please write this seed phrase on paper and store it securely.

Once your wallet is set up, transferring cryptocurrencies to it is a breeze.

Connect your hardware wallet to your computer and open the corresponding software.

From here, you can send your digital assets from an exchange or another wallet to your cold wallet's public address.

If you ever need to receive funds, give the sender your public address—never your private key. Your public address acts like a bank account number, and it is safe to share with others to receive funds.

To find your public address, open your wallet software and navigate to the 'Receive' or 'Deposit' section; the address will usually be displayed as a long string of characters or a QR code.

If you're using an exchange, log in to your account, go to the wallet or funds section, and select the cryptocurrency you wish to receive. From there, look for the 'Deposit' button to display your public address for that specific coin.

Maintaining the security of your cold wallet is an ongoing process.

Regularly check for firmware updates from the manufacturer. These updates often contain important security patches that protect against new threats.

You should store your backup seed phrase in a safe location, separate from your wallet, to prevent both from being compromised simultaneously.

Consider using a fireproof safe or a safety deposit box for added protection.

Avoid exposing your cold wallet to the internet or malicious software. Only connect it to trusted devices and networks to minimize risks.

Incorporating these best practices will help you safeguard your cryptocurrency, allowing you to rest easy knowing your digital assets are secure.

Cold wallets offer robust protection for long-term storage, making them an integral part of a comprehensive cryptocurrency security strategy.

Software Updates

Regular **software updates** are akin to fortifying your digital defenses.

Just as you'd update your antivirus software to protect against new viruses, keeping your wallet software and exchange apps up-to-date is crucial.

Developers frequently release updates to patch vulnerabilities and enhance security features.

Many overlook this step, yet it's vital for maintaining the integrity of your crypto assets.

Similarly, ensure that the operating systems on devices you use for trading are regularly updated. This minimizes the risk of malware or other malicious software compromising your security.

Security Checklist for Cryptocurrency Investors

- Store seed phrases securely offline; avoid digital copies.

- Use a reputable password manager for strong, unique passwords.

- Enable multifactor authentication on all crypto accounts.

- Use a hardware wallet like Ledger or Trezor for offline storage.

- Regularly update wallet software and exchange apps.

- Keep device operating systems updated to prevent vulnerabilities.

Implementing these security practices builds a robust defense against potential threats. This proactive approach protects your assets and offers peace of mind.

Avoiding Scams: Identifying Red Flags

Opportunities abound in the vast and exciting world of cryptocurrency, but so do potential pitfalls. Just as in any new frontier, some seek to exploit the unwary.

Scams in the crypto space come in various guises, each more cunning than the last.

One of the most prevalent is the **phishing attack**, a digital con where scammers pose as reputable entities to trick you into revealing sensitive information like your login credentials or private keys.

These attacks often come via email or text, with messages that look official but contain malicious links.

Clicking on these can lead to stolen information or access to your crypto wallets.

Another common scam is the **Ponzi scheme**, where fraudulent platforms promise high returns using new investors' money to pay earlier backers.

These schemes rely on continuous recruitment and eventually collapse, leaving most participants in the lurch.

Then there are **fake wallet and exchange apps** that mimic legitimate ones, designed to steal your funds once you input your details.

So, how do you safeguard yourself amidst these threats?

A critical step is verifying the legitimacy of any crypto project or exchange before investing.

Start by checking for regulatory compliance and licenses. Legitimate exchanges and projects usually operate under the supervision of relevant authorities and provide proof of registration.

Research the project team as well. Transparency is key; trustworthy ventures openly share information about their team members, backgrounds, and previous projects.

If a project is cagey about who is behind it, consider that a red flag.

Look for a well-documented white paper that outlines the project's purpose, technology, and roadmap. This document should be clear and detailed, not just marketing fluff.

Keep your eyes peeled for warning signs indicating a scheme designed to separate you from your money.

Promises of guaranteed high returns should set off alarm bells. In the unpredictable realm of crypto, no legitimate investment can guarantee profits.

Be wary of pressure tactics urging immediate investment. Scammers often create a false sense of urgency to rush you into making hasty decisions.

If a project lacks verifiable information or a detailed white paper, it's wise to steer clear.

Transparency is a hallmark of credible ventures; any lack thereof signals to dig deeper or walk away.

Staying safe online requires a proactive approach. Avoid oversharing private information on social media platforms, where scammers often scout for potential targets.

Use secure, unique passwords for each account to prevent a breach from affecting multiple platforms.

Reusing passwords for convenience is tempting, but doing so makes it easier for cybercriminals to access your accounts.

Always scrutinize emails and messages that ask for personal information or direct you to websites. Trust your instincts and verify the source before clicking links if something seems off.

In the crypto community, knowledge is your best armor. Keep informed about the latest scams and tactics used by cybercriminals.

Reading up on others' experiences can provide valuable lessons and help you recognize potential threats before falling prey to them.

Join online forums or groups to share insights and stay up-dated on new developments. Engaging with a community of like-minded individuals can offer support and camaraderie in a landscape that is as exhilarating as it is challenging.

Remember, while the promise of cryptocurrency is vast, so is the need for vigilance.

Risk Management: Strategies for Volatile Markets

Cryptocurrency is known for its wild volatility, which can be a double-edged sword.

It's like riding a roller coaster where the highs can be exhila-rating, but the lows are stomach-churning.

In this world, prices can swing dramatically quickly, driven by factors like market sentiment, news, or even tweets from influential personalities.

This unpredictability means that while you might see impres-sive gains, you could also face significant losses.

Market corrections, where prices adjust after a rapid rise, can catch investors off guard. It's essential to manage your emotions and not let fear or greed dictate your decisions.

Staying cool-headed is crucial, especially when the market seems to be in a frenzy.

One way to navigate this unpredictability is by employing risk management strategies to protect your investments.

Dollar-cost averaging is a technique where you invest a fixed amount of money at regular intervals, regardless of the asset's price.

This approach smooths out the price volatility, as you buy more when prices are low and less when they're high.

It's a disciplined method that reduces the impact of price swings and takes the guesswork out of timing the market.

Another strategy is setting **stop-loss orders**, which automatically sell an asset when its price drops to a certain level.

This acts as a safety net, limiting potential losses and protecting your portfolio from catastrophic declines.

While stop-loss orders can be a useful tool for protecting your investment, use them cautiously.

In the volatile world of cryptocurrency, a sudden price dip might trigger your stop-loss, preventing further losses—but it could also cause you to miss out on an inevitable rebound when the coin bounces back.

Diversifying your investments across multiple cryptocurrencies is also a wise way to manage your risk.

By spreading your assets, you reduce risk exposure to any single coin's volatility. This diversification means that if one asset performs poorly, others may balance your overall portfolio.

Stablecoins also play a pivotal role in risk management, providing a safe haven during turbulent times.

As we discussed, these digital currencies are pegged to a stable asset, like the US dollar, which helps maintain their value despite market fluctuations.

Converting some of your holdings to stablecoins can preserve your wealth in times of uncertainty.

They serve as a buffer, reducing your portfolio's exposure to the extreme volatility of other cryptocurrencies.

Allocating a portion of your investments to stablecoins can add a layer of stability, allowing you to weather market storms with less anxiety.

Creating a risk management plan involves aligning your investment strategy with personal goals and risk tolerance.

Start by assessing how much risk you're comfortable taking. Are you a risk-taker who can handle the market's ups and downs, or do you prefer a more conservative approach?

This self-assessment will guide your investment choices and risk management tactics.

Regularly reviewing and adjusting your strategy is also essential. Markets evolve, and so should your plan.

Make it a habit to periodically evaluate your portfolio, ensuring it aligns with your financial goals and risk tolerance.

Maintaining a long-term perspective is key to mitigating short-term volatility. Focus on your end goals and avoid getting caught up in daily market noise.

A steady approach helps you stay grounded, making informed decisions based on logic rather than emotion.

In the grand tapestry of investing, risk management is your safety net. It allows you to pursue the potential of cryptocurrencies while safeguarding your assets from unnecessary risk.

Keep these strategies in mind as you continue to build your crypto portfolio. They'll help you navigate the market's inherent volatility and position you for long-term success.

With a solid risk management plan in place, you can focus on exploring cryptocurrency's opportunities, confident in your ability to handle whatever the market throws your way.

As we move forward, let's explore advanced tools and resources that can enhance your crypto journey, providing you with the knowledge and skills to make informed decisions.

Advanced Tools and Resources

Imagine having a personal assistant who never sleeps, constantly scanning the markets and making trades on your behalf, all while you go about your daily life.

This is the promise of **trading bots**, a fascinating innovation in cryptocurrency.

What is a Trading Bot?

These digital assistants are designed to automate the buying and selling of cryptocurrencies based on pre-set parameters, taking some of the pressure off your shoulders.

The primary advantage of trading bots is their ability to operate 24/7, tirelessly monitoring market conditions and executing trades even while you sleep.

This constant vigilance can be incredibly helpful, especially in a market that never closes.

Another significant benefit is the reduction of emotional decision-making. By sticking to programmed strategies, trading bots help you avoid the common pitfalls of panic selling or buying on impulse, ensuring that your investment decisions remain consistent and rational.

However, using trading bots isn't without its risks and considerations.

One potential pitfall is overfitting, where the bot is too closely aligned with past data, potentially leading to poor performance in changing market conditions.

It's essential to regularly monitor your bot's performance and make adjustments as necessary.

Another consideration is the security of your API connections. Ensure you use strong, unique passwords and enable two-factor authentication to protect your account from unauthorized access.

Regular oversight is essential, as markets can shift rapidly, and what worked yesterday may not be effective tomorrow.

For this reason, I recommend **NOT** attempting bot trading until you have furthered your education on the topic.

While bot trading might seem like an effortless way to earn profits, the reality is that many bots fall short of their promises, often leading to more losses than manual trading.

The real issue usually lies in the bot software you select and your understanding of how to configure and adjust them effectively.

As markets shift, your bot settings must adapt, too, and covering every possible scenario in this book isn't feasible.

That's why I highly recommend an exceptional course called *The Plan* by Dan Hollings.

His training on bot trading is the most comprehensive and easy to follow that I have ever seen, making him my go-to expert on this topic.

One of the best parts of his course is the continuous updates he provides on the most effective bots and settings for current market conditions—at no additional cost.

If you're serious about mastering bot trading, I've included a link to his course on the resources page I've created for this book.

SCAN ME!

Or visit
ArthurBellBooks.com/crypto.html
for **Helpful Resources** Related to
this book!

Within this realm of automation, several platforms stand out for their unique offerings.

One such platform is **3Commas**, known for its customizable trading strategies. It allows you to tailor your trading approach to fit your personal risk tolerance and investment goals.

With features like trailing stop loss and smart cover options, 3Commas empowers you to manage your trades precisely.

Another popular choice is **HaasOnline**, which offers a suite of technical analysis tools. These tools enable you to build sophisticated trading strategies, incorporating indicators and signals to refine your approach.

Then there's **Cryptohopper**, a cloud-based solution that offers the convenience of managing your trades from anywhere. With its strategy designer tool, you can backtest your ideas before deploying them, ensuring that your strategies are practical and aligned with market conditions.

Setting up a trading bot involves a few key steps that require careful consideration.

First, using API keys, you must connect your trading bot to your chosen exchange. These keys allow the bot to access your account and execute trades on your behalf.

It's crucial to ensure that these API connections are secure, as they are the gateway to your assets.

Once connected, you'll adjust the bot's parameters and risk settings to match your investment strategy. This might include defining your stop-loss levels or setting specific conditions under which the bot will buy or sell.

The beauty of these settings is that they allow you to automate your strategy while retaining control over key decisions.

Evaluating Trading Bot Effectiveness

- **Consider the primary goal of using a trading bot:** Is your goal to save time, reduce emotional decisions, or improve trade accuracy?

- **Reflect on how your bot's performance aligns with your financial goals:** Are the trades it executes meeting your expectations?

- Identify any necessary adjustments in strategies or risk settings to optimize performance.

Trading bots offer an exciting opportunity to enhance your cryptocurrency trading strategy.

By automating repetitive tasks and allowing you to maintain a consistent approach, they can be a valuable asset in your investment toolkit.

Yet, like any tool, they require understanding and oversight. As you explore the world of trading bots, remember to approach them with an open mind and a willingness to learn.

With the proper setup and careful monitoring, they can help you confidently navigate the dynamic landscape of cryptocurrency trading.

Leveraging Online Communities for Support and Insight

Navigating the vast, ever-evolving world of cryptocurrency can sometimes feel like trying to solve a puzzle with missing pieces.

But here's where online communities come in, acting as a valuable resource where you can find those missing pieces.

Engaging with like-minded individuals provides insights and support that can be both enlightening and encouraging.

These communities are filled with people who have been where you are now, eager to share their experiences and advice.

This collaborative environment is a goldmine for learning, where you can stay updated on market trends and gain perspectives you might not have considered.

Popular platforms like **Reddit's r/cryptocurrency** offer a space for diverse discussions. You'll find everything from beginner questions to in-depth analyses catering to various interests and expertise levels here.

This subreddit is like a bustling town square where ideas are exchanged freely.

BitcoinTalk, on the other hand, is the go-to forum for more technical discussions. It's where you can dive deep into the intricacies of blockchain technology and get technical advice from seasoned experts.

For those who prefer real-time communication, **Telegram groups** provide instant interaction. These groups are vibrant communities where news and insights are shared at light-ning speed, keeping you in the loop with the latest develop-ments. However, these groups typically charge a fee to be a member.

To make the most of these online interactions, it's vital to participate. Start by asking informed questions. Engage in discussions with curiosity and a willingness to learn.

This helps you gain knowledge and builds your credibility within the community.

When you have insights or knowledge to share, contribute to the conversation. Your experiences might offer valuable lessons to others, fostering a supportive network where members can rely on each other.

Always adhere to community guidelines and etiquette, as respecting these norms creates a welcoming atmosphere for everyone involved.

However, the open nature of these communities means that misinformation can spread easily.

To protect yourself, it's crucial to be discerning.

Cross-reference information from multiple sources before accepting it as truth. This helps counteract the spread of false or misleading advice.

Be especially cautious of unverified tips or investment advice, sometimes based on speculation rather than fact.

Learning to recognize the difference between opinion and fact is key. Opinions can provide interesting perspectives, but facts grounded in data and research are what you want to base your decisions on.

That said, while online communities offer a wealth of information, they can also be overwhelming and full of distractions.

It's easy to get lost in endless debates or recommendations to invest in coins that might not align with your goals.

This is why I strongly encourage finding a trusted expert to follow—someone who can cut through the noise and provide reliable, up-to-date advice.

For me, that person is Dan Hollings, the creator of the course *The Plan.* His guidance on cryptocurrency and bot trading has been invaluable.

Dan's advice is based on thorough research and practical experience, and he consistently provides updates tailored to current market conditions.

By following someone like Dan, you can focus on actionable strategies and avoid wasting time on irrelevant or speculative discussions.

I've included a link to his course on the resources page for anyone interested.

SCAN ME!

Or visit
ArthurBellBooks.com/crypto.html
for **Helpful Resources** Related to
this book!

However, online communities offer a support system where you can celebrate successes and work through challenges together.

You can enhance your understanding and confidence in cryptocurrency investing by engaging actively and thoughtfully.

These communities become a lifeline, providing the insights and encouragement needed to thrive in a complex and dynamic environment.

As you immerse yourself in these spaces, remember to approach each interaction with an open mind and a critical eye, ensuring you get the most accurate and valuable information possible.

As we close this chapter, it's clear that leveraging technology and community can significantly enhance your crypto experience.

These advanced tools and resources empower you to make informed decisions, protect your investments, and connect with others.

Next, we'll explore the legal and ethical considerations essential to responsible crypto investing, helping you navigate the regulatory landscape with confidence and integrity.

Legal and Ethical Considerations

Let me take you back to a moment not too long ago when I found myself at a conference buzzing with excitement.

The air was thick with the promise of innovation. Yet, there was a palpable tension—a reminder that the crypto world, as thrilling as it is, is governed by an intricate web of rules and regulations.

I recall chatting with a fellow investor grappling with the complexities of global regulations. It struck me then how essential it is for anyone venturing into cryptocurrency to understand the legal landscape.

Whether you're a young adult just starting, an adult looking to diversify, or a senior exploring new opportunities, knowing the rules of the game is crucial.

Understanding the current regulatory landscape for cryptocurrencies globally can feel like walking through a maze. Each country has crafted its own set of rules, reflecting diverse attitudes towards digital currencies.

In the United States, regulatory bodies like the Securities and Exchange Commission (SEC) play a significant role in overseeing Initial Coin Offerings (ICOs) and classifying them as securities.

Many crypto projects must comply with stringent regulations similar to those governing traditional financial products.

The European Union, meanwhile, has embraced a more unified approach with the Markets in Crypto-Assets (MiCA) regulation, aiming to create a harmonized framework across member states.

This regulation seeks to protect investors while fostering innovation, a delicate balance pivotal for the crypto market's growth.

In Asia, the approach varies greatly from country to country.

Once a central hub for crypto mining, China has imposed strict bans, driving miners to seek refuge in more welcoming jurisdictions.

Meanwhile, Japan and South Korea have adopted progressive stances, implementing robust regulatory frameworks to ensure the safety and transparency of cryptocurrency transactions.

Some countries, like Switzerland and Singapore, are known for their crypto-friendly policies. These nations have positioned themselves as global leaders by creating environments conducive to blockchain innovation, attracting businesses and investors alike.

Regulations impact how cryptocurrencies are traded and the operations of exchanges and ICOs.

Compliance with **Know Your Customer (KYC)** and **Anti-Money Laundering (AML)** requirements is mandatory, ensuring that exchanges verify the identities of their users and monitor transactions for suspicious activity.

This is crucial for maintaining the financial system's integrity and preventing illicit activities.

The SEC's regulations in the U.S. have clarified the classification of cryptocurrencies, offering guidance on what constitutes a security. This has profound implications for ICOs, as projects must understand these rules to avoid legal pitfalls.

Government policies significantly shape the crypto market, influencing investor behavior and market dynamics.

In recent years, we've seen both encouraging incentives and restrictive measures.

Some governments offer tax incentives to blockchain companies, encouraging technological advancements and economic growth. These incentives can be a boon for startups looking to innovate without the burden of heavy taxation.

On the flip side, bans on crypto mining in certain regions have forced miners to relocate, impacting the global distribution of mining activity.

Such bans often stem from environmental concerns or the desire to control capital flows, reflecting the complex interplay between regulation and market forces.

Staying compliant with global regulations requires vigilance and proactive measures. Keeping abreast of regulatory updates is essential, as the legal landscape can shift rapidly.

Subscribing to trusted news sources and participating in industry forums can help you stay informed.

When dealing with cross-border transactions, consulting with legal professionals can provide clarity and ensure compliance with international standards.

This is particularly important for those looking to tap into global markets or who are involved in international trading.

By approaching the crypto market with an informed perspective, you can confidently negotiate the complexities of regulation and focus on building a secure and successful investment portfolio.

Tax Implications of Cryptocurrency Investments

Picture this: you've just executed a successful trade, your digital portfolio is flourishing, and you feel on top of the world.

But before you pop the champagne, there's an important aspect to consider—taxes.

Like traditional investments, cryptocurrency activities come with tax obligations that vary depending on the type of transaction.

In the United States, for instance, the IRS treats cryptocurrencies as property, meaning each sale or trade is a taxable event subject to capital gains tax.

This means if you sell your Bitcoin for a profit, you'll owe taxes on the gain.

The same goes for trading one cryptocurrency for another or using crypto to make purchases.

The tax rate you pay depends on how long you've held the asset: short-term gains (held for less than a year) are taxed at regular income rates, while long-term gains (held for more than a year) benefit from reduced rates.

Beyond trading, activities like mining and staking have their own tax implications.

When you mine cryptocurrency, the value of the coins at the time of receipt is considered taxable income. This can significantly affect your tax bill, especially if you're a prolific miner.

Similarly, rewards from staking—where you earn crypto by participating in a network's operations—are taxable as income.

Understanding these obligations is crucial to avoid unexpected liabilities and stay on the right side of the law.

Keeping accurate records of your transactions is not just good practice—it's essential. Every time you trade, sell, or earn cryptocurrency, you're creating a tax event, and you'll need to document it.

This involves tracking your transaction history and the cost basis of your assets, which is the original value of the crypto when you acquired it. This forms the basis for calculating gains or losses when you sell.

Given the complexity and volume of transactions, using crypto tax software can be a lifesaver. Tools like **CoinLedger** integrate with exchanges and wallets, automating the tracking process and generating tax reports that simplify filing.

The tax landscape for cryptocurrencies isn't uniform across the globe. While the U.S. requires meticulous reporting, some countries like Portugal offer more lenient treatment.

In Portugal, individuals can enjoy tax-free crypto transactions, making it an attractive destination for crypto enthusiasts. However, this isn't the case everywhere.

Some jurisdictions impose strict regulations, requiring detailed reporting and compliance.

In the U.S., the IRS has ramped up enforcement, even requiring exchanges to issue Form 1099-DA starting in 2025 to report gains and losses.

Reducing your tax liabilities legally requires strategic planning. One effective method is holding your assets for more than a year to qualify for long-term capital gains tax rates.

These rates are typically lower than short-term rates, which can significantly decrease your tax burden.

Another strategy is **tax-loss harvesting**, where you sell underperforming assets at a loss to offset gains elsewhere in your portfolio.

This can be particularly useful during market downturns, allowing you to decrease your taxable income.

It's important to remember that while the potential for profit in cryptocurrency is exciting, staying compliant with tax laws is critical. Ignoring these obligations can result in penalties and fines, overshadowing any financial gains.

Maneuvering the tax implications of cryptocurrency can feel overwhelming. Still, with the proper knowledge and tools, you can confidently manage your responsibilities.

By staying informed and proactive, you can focus on what matters most—growing your investments and exploring the opportunities that the world of cryptocurrency has to offer.

Ethical Investing: Aligning Crypto with Your Values

Ethical investing in cryptocurrency is a concept that resonates deeply with many of us. It's about aligning your financial activities with your personal beliefs and values.

In the crypto space, this means looking beyond potential profits to evaluate your investments' impact on society and the environment.

Transparency and **accountability** are two fundamental principles to consider.

In a world where anonymity often reigns, ethical investors seek projects that operate with openness. This involves scrutinizing how transparent a project is about its operations, funding, and future plans.

Accountability is crucial, too. Projects that hold themselves responsible for their actions and outcomes are more likely to earn your trust and support.

The environment is another key aspect of ethical investing.

Cryptocurrency mining, particularly Bitcoin, is notorious for its heavy energy consumption. This has sparked debates about the sustainability of digital currencies.

As an investor, consider how your investments impact the planet.

Some blockchain technologies are taking steps towards environmental sustainability.

For example, Ethereum's transition to Ethereum 2.0, which utilizes a Proof of Stake (PoS) consensus mechanism, significantly reduces energy consumption compared to the traditional Proof of Work (PoW) system.

Supporting projects prioritizing eco-friendly practices can align your portfolio with your environmental values, allowing you to contribute to a greener future while pursuing financial growth.

The environmental impact of crypto mining is a pressing concern for many investors. Bitcoin mining, for instance, consumes a staggering amount of energy.

Reports indicate that the energy used for mining in one year can rival the electricity consumption of entire countries. This raises significant ecological questions.

However, potential solutions are emerging. As mentioned, Ethereum 2.0 represents a shift towards more sustainable blockchain solutions.

Other projects are exploring renewable energy sources for mining operations, which could mitigate some of the environmental damage.

As an investor, supporting these forward-thinking initiatives can contribute to a more sustainable crypto ecosystem.

Aligning investments with personal values also means seeking out projects with a positive social impact.

This could be anything from initiatives that promote financial inclusion in underserved communities to those that support renewable energy solutions.

These projects often aim to make a meaningful difference in the world, and by investing in them, you're not just chasing profits—you're contributing to a cause you believe in.

Conversely, it also involves steering clear of projects with questionable practices. Those that lack transparency, have dubious governance structures, or are engaged in unethical activities should raise red flags.

In doing so, you protect both your investments and your principles.

When evaluating the ethical standards of crypto projects, consider examining the governance structures of decentralized organizations.

These structures dictate how decisions are made and how power is distributed within the project.

For example, **Decentralized Autonomous Organizations (DAOs)** often operate on democratic principles, giving stakeholders a voice in decision-making. This can be a positive sign of ethical governance.

Additionally, assess the transparency of project teams and their development practices. Teams that openly communicate their goals, challenges, and progress are more likely to foster trust and demonstrate a commitment to ethical standards.

Look for projects that publish regular updates and engage with their communities. This transparency builds credibility and allows you, as an investor, to make informed decisions.

Incorporating ethical considerations into your investment strategy can enhance your personal satisfaction and contribute to positive change. It allows you to take an active role in shaping the future of the crypto industry, guiding it towards practices that align with your values.

Remember that ethical investing is a personal journey. It's about balancing financial returns and the impact you wish to have on the world.

Next, we'll examine the real-world applications of cryptocurrencies, offering insights into how digital assets are transforming industries and economies worldwide.

Make a Difference with Your Review

"Knowledge shared is knowledge multiplied." – *Robert Noyce*

You've taken a big step by reading *Cryptocurrency Investing for Beginners: The Ultimate 30-Day Step-by-Step Guide to Easily & Safely Invest in Crypto, Build Wealth, and Avoid Costly Mistakes—Even if You're Starting from Zero.*

Now, I'd love your help making this journey easier for others.

Imagine someone like you who is curious about cryptocurrency but hesitant to dive in.

Your review could encourage them to take that first step toward financial freedom.

Why Your Review Matters

Most people rely on reviews to decide which book to trust.

By leaving your honest feedback, you're not just helping me—you're helping someone else start their crypto journey with confidence.

Your review could inspire:

- Someone to finally set up their first crypto wallet.

- A new investor to avoid costly mistakes.

- A curious learner to feel empowered instead of intimidated by the crypto world.

How to Leave a Review

It's easy, free, and takes just a minute!

1. Visit https://www.amazon.com/review/review-your -purchases/?asin=B0DSC1LR72 or scan the QR code below.

2. Share your thoughts—what you loved, what helped you, or anything you think future readers should know.

Your words can make a world of difference.

Thank You

If this book has helped you, your review is the best way to pay it forward.

Thank you for being part of this growing community of crypto investors.

Your support means the world to me!

Warmly,

Arthur Bell

Case Studies and Real-World Applications

Imagine being just a teenager and stepping into a world that most adults find daunting. That's precisely what Erik Finman did.

At just 12 years old, Erik received a $1,000 gift from his grandmother, which he decided to invest in Bitcoin.

It was 2011, and Bitcoin was still a relatively obscure digital currency, but Erik saw potential where others didn't.

By the time Bitcoin reached its zenith, his modest investment had ballooned into over a million dollars, transforming him into one of the youngest self-made millionaires.

What set Erik apart was his willingness to leap into the unknown, armed with curiosity and a desire to learn.

He didn't just rely on Bitcoin; he diversified his portfolio, exploring other cryptocurrencies like Ether, even though he remained skeptical about some aspects of the crypto market.

Erik's story isn't just about making money; it's about the courage to explore new frontiers and the vision to see what others might overlook.

Then there are the Winklevoss twins, Cameron and Tyler, whose foresight and determination helped shape the cryptocurrency landscape.

Known for their legal battle with Mark Zuckerberg over the founding of Facebook, the twins shifted their focus to Bitcoin, seeing it as the next big thing.

They invested early, amassing one of the largest Bitcoin portfolios in the world. Their belief in Bitcoin was unwavering, even during times of market uncertainty.

They championed the idea of Bitcoin as a new form of money, not just a speculative asset. Through their investment firm, they supported the development of a robust Bitcoin ecosystem, contributing to the currency's broader acceptance and growth.

So, what were the strategies and decisions that fueled these successes?

Both Erik Finman and the Winklevoss twins employed a mix of long-term holding and strategic diversification.

Erik's youthful enthusiasm led him to hold onto his Bitcoin through its volatile early years while branching out into other promising cryptocurrencies.

On the other hand, the twins combined their long-term commitment to Bitcoin with investments in related technologies and businesses that supported the crypto ecosystem.

They understood the importance of diversification—not just within their cryptocurrency holdings but also in their investment approach, supporting the infrastructure needed for Bitcoin's success.

Timing and market conditions played a pivotal role in these success stories.

Erik's early entry into the Bitcoin market allowed him to capitalize on the currency's explosive growth during its early adoption phase. He was positioned perfectly to benefit from Bitcoin's bull market cycles, where prices surged dramatically.

Similarly, the Winklevoss twins invested when Bitcoin was gaining traction but had not yet achieved mainstream recognition. Their early adoption allowed them to ride the wave of Bitcoin's increasing popularity and value.

These investors understood the importance of being ahead of the curve and recognizing opportunities before they became evident to the broader market.

We can extract valuable lessons from these stories for our investment strategies. Staying informed and updated on market trends is crucial.

Erik Finman and the Winklevoss twins were both well-versed in the developments within the cryptocurrency space, allowing them to make informed decisions.

As a crypto investor, keeping abreast of the latest news, technological advancements, and regulatory changes can give you insights into navigating the market effectively.

Moreover, learning from early adopters and their innovative approaches can inspire you to think outside the box and explore new opportunities.

These stories remind us that success often comes from a mix of courage, knowledge, and strategic action. By applying these lessons, you can better position yourself to seize the opportunities within the dynamic world of cryptocurrency.

Cautionary Tales: Lessons from Failed Investments

Imagine the excitement of discovering a new investment opportunity, only to have it unravel into a nightmare.

This was the unfortunate reality for many involved with BitConnect, a platform that promised astronomical returns through its "Lending Program."

Investors were lured by claims of earning significant profits using BitConnect's proprietary trading bot and volatility software.

At its peak, BitConnect reached a market cap of $3.4 billion, painting a picture of success.

But the facade soon crumbled. It turned out to be a classic Ponzi scheme, where returns were paid using new investors' funds rather than legitimate profits.

The collapse left countless investors reeling from their losses, their dreams dashed by the harsh truth of deceit. This saga is a stark reminder of the dangers lurking in crypto, where too-good-to-be-true schemes can lead to financial ruin.

Another cautionary tale is the infamous Mt. Gox hack, which shook the Bitcoin community to its core.

Once the largest Bitcoin exchange, handling over 70% of all Bitcoin transactions worldwide, Mt. Gox was considered a pillar of the crypto world. Investors trusted the platform with their assets, believing in its security and reliability.

However, in 2014, a catastrophic breach occurred, resulting in the theft of approximately 850,000 Bitcoins.

The fallout was devastating, not only for the investors who lost their funds but also for the cryptocurrency market as a whole.

The incident exposed significant vulnerabilities within the exchange and highlighted the pressing need for robust security measures.

The collapse of Mt. Gox eroded trust in centralized exchanges, raising questions about the safety and stability of the crypto market.

What went wrong with BitConnect and Mt. Gox? A common thread in these failures was a lack of due diligence.

Many investors were swept up by the hype surrounding Initial Coin Offerings (ICOs) and new platforms, neglecting to research the projects they were investing in thoroughly. This oversight left them vulnerable to scams and fraudulent schemes.

Another pitfall was over-leveraging—investors poured more money than they could afford to lose into these ventures, betting on promises of high returns without considering the risks involved.

In the case of Mt. Gox, inadequate risk management and security protocols allowed a breach to occur, underscoring the importance of safeguarding assets against cyber threats.

The consequences of these failures were profound, shaking investor confidence and prompting calls for greater oversight.

The loss of funds and trust in centralized exchanges led to increased scrutiny from regulators. This push for stricter regulations aimed to protect investors and prevent similar incidents from occurring in the future.

As the market grappled with these challenges, it became clear that a more cautious, informed approach was necessary to navigate the volatile world of cryptocurrency.

Learning from these cautionary tales, there are valuable lessons to be gleaned.

First and foremost, conducting thorough research before investing in any project is vital. Understand the fundamentals, evaluate the development team, and scrutinize the project's goals and execution strategy.

This diligence can help identify red flags and protect against scams.

Diversification is another critical strategy I continue to mention because it is so important.

By spreading investments across multiple assets, you reduce exposure to any single point of failure. This approach not only mitigates risk but also enhances the potential for returns by capturing opportunities across different sectors of the market.

Ultimately, these stories serve as cautionary reminders of the potential pitfalls in the crypto world. They emphasize the need for vigilance, due diligence, and sound investment strategies to negotiate the market's complexities.

Cryptocurrency's Impact on Global Finance

Cryptocurrencies have dramatically altered the landscape of global finance, offering a new way to think about money and transactions.

One of the most significant changes is the emergence of blockchain-based remittances, which have revolutionized how people send money across borders.

Traditionally, cross-border payments were slow and expensive, often burdened by hefty fees and delays. However, these transfers are now faster, more secure, and far more affordable with cryptocurrencies.

This shift is particularly beneficial for individuals in developing countries who rely on remittances from family members working abroad. The reduced costs and increased speed make a tangible difference in their lives, providing them with more resources to support their families.

Beyond remittances, **decentralized finance**, or **DeFi**, is reshaping financial services.

DeFi platforms leverage blockchain technology to offer alternatives to traditional banking products. Imagine accessing loans, earning interest, or trading assets without ever setting foot in a bank.

That's the promise of DeFi. These platforms eliminate inter-mediaries, reduce fees, and make financial services more accessible.

They offer a democratized approach to finance, where any-one with an internet connection can participate.

This innovation is shifting how we think about finance and who gets to participate in it. DeFi is opening doors for those who have long been excluded from the traditional financial system.

Cryptocurrencies also drive financial inclusion, providing ac-cess to banking services for underserved populations.

In many developing regions, traditional banking infrastruc-ture is either lacking or inaccessible to a significant portion of the population.

Cryptocurrencies offer a solution by enabling peer-to-peer transactions, allowing individuals to send and receive money directly.

This capability is empowering people who have never had access to a bank account, giving them control over their finances for the first time.

With just a smartphone, they can engage in financial activi-ties that were previously out of reach. This empowerment is a strong force for economic growth and stability, as it brings more people into the formal financial system.

The rise of cryptocurrencies presents both challenges and opportunities for central banks and governments.

As digital currencies gain traction, traditional financial institutions are rethinking their roles.

Central bank digital currencies (CBDCs) have emerged as a response to the growing popularity of cryptocurrencies. These digital versions of national currencies aim to combine the efficiency of digital transactions with the stability of government-backed money.

However, implementing CBDCs is not without its hurdles. Balancing innovation with consumer protection is a delicate act.

Regulators face the challenge of creating frameworks that foster innovation while safeguarding against fraud and money laundering risks. This balancing act is crucial for integrating cryptocurrencies into the broader financial ecosystem.

Real-world applications of cryptocurrencies are already evident across various sectors.

Bitcoin, for example, has become a popular store of value in times of economic instability. In countries with hyperinflation or political unrest, people turn to Bitcoin to preserve their wealth.

Its decentralized nature and limited supply make it an attractive alternative to unstable national currencies.

Meanwhile, Ethereum's smart contracts automate business processes, reduce costs, and increase efficiency. These self-executing contracts eliminate the need for intermediaries, streamlining complex transactions in industries like real estate and finance.

Furthermore, blockchain technology is enhancing supply chain transparency and efficiency. By providing a tamper-proof record of transactions, blockchain ensures the authenticity of goods. It reduces fraud, benefiting both businesses and consumers.

The transformative effect of cryptocurrencies on global finance is undeniable. They are reshaping existing systems and creating new opportunities for individuals and businesses alike.

This chapter highlights the expansive reach of cryptocurrencies, showing how they influence everything from personal finance to international trade.

As we continue to explore the world of crypto, it's clear that these digital currencies are more than just a financial trend—they are a fundamental shift in how we understand and interact with money.

In the next chapter, we'll delve into the integration of cryptocurrency with traditional investments, exploring how you can blend these new opportunities with established financial strategies.

Integrating Crypto with Traditional Investments

Cryptocurrencies offer exciting growth potential, while traditional investment vehicles like Roth IRAs provide stability and long-term security.

By combining these two, you can build a diversified portfolio that leverages the best of both worlds.

This approach allows you to benefit from the growth of digital assets while taking advantage of the tax benefits of a retirement account.

Cryptocurrency and Roth IRAs: Setting Up for Success

Investing in cryptocurrency through a Roth IRA is like planting seeds in fertile ground.

You're setting yourself up for tax-free growth, meaning any profits you make from your investments won't be taxed when you withdraw them in retirement.

This is a significant advantage, especially in the volatile world of cryptocurrency, where gains can be substantial.

A Roth IRA is designed for long-term wealth building, aligning perfectly with the growth prospects of cryptocurrencies.

By incorporating digital assets into your retirement account, you're diversifying your portfolio and positioning yourself for potential future gains.

However, the legal and regulatory framework for crypto IRAs requires careful maneuvering.

According to the IRS, while cryptocurrencies are permissible within IRAs, they classify them as property, not currency. This distinction impacts how they're taxed and managed.

To invest in crypto through a Roth IRA, you need a self-directed IRA, which allows for a broader range of investments beyond traditional stocks and bonds.

Not all IRAs support cryptocurrency, so finding a custodian specializing in crypto IRAs is essential.

These custodians ensure compliance with IRS regulations, offering security and peace of mind as you diversify your retirement savings.

Setting up a crypto Roth IRA involves several steps, beginning with choosing a reputable custodian.

Companies like **BitcoinIRA** or **iTrustCapital** are examples of custodians that facilitate crypto investments.

They offer services tailored to digital assets, including secure storage and comprehensive account management.

Once you've selected a custodian, the next step is funding your account. You can do this by rolling over existing retirement funds from a traditional IRA or 401(k) or making new contributions.

It's a straightforward process, but it's wise to consult with a financial advisor to understand the implications and ensure compliance with tax laws.

The benefits of including cryptocurrencies in your Roth IRA are compelling, yet it's crucial to consider the potential drawbacks.

On the positive side, cryptocurrencies can provide diversification within your retirement portfolio. They offer exposure to a high-growth asset class distinct from traditional investments.

This diversification can enhance your portfolio's resilience, helping to buffer against market downturns in conventional assets.

However, cryptocurrencies are known for their volatility. Prices fluctuate wildly, which might not suit everyone, especially those nearing retirement who prefer more stable investments.

Additionally, the security of digital assets is paramount. While custodians offer protective measures, understanding and mitigating risks is crucial.

Evaluating Crypto Roth IRAs

- **Assess your risk tolerance:** How comfortable are you with the volatility of cryptocurrencies within a retirement account?

- **Consider your investment timeline:** Does the long-term growth potential of crypto align with your retirement goals?

- **Research custodians:** Compare services, fees, and security measures to find the best fit for your needs.

As you explore this exciting intersection of traditional and digital finance, carefully weigh the risks and rewards, ensuring that your investment strategy aligns with your financial goals and comfort level.

Balancing Crypto with Stocks and Bonds

Cryptocurrencies, with their dynamic risk-return profile, differ significantly from traditional assets.

While stocks and bonds offer a stable, predictable path, digital currencies present a more volatile yet potentially rewarding journey.

This contrast makes cryptocurrencies an exciting addition to a diversified portfolio, providing opportunities for enhanced returns while spreading risk across different asset classes.

Exploring how cryptocurrencies behave compared to stocks and bonds reveals intriguing patterns.

Historically, stocks and bonds have shown varying degrees of correlation during market downturns, often moving in tandem to some extent.

On the other hand, cryptocurrencies usually operate independently of these traditional assets.

This lack of correlation means that digital assets might not be affected similarly when markets face turmoil, offering a potential hedge against broader market volatility.

Such behavior provides a strategic advantage when constructing a portfolio, allowing investors to mitigate risks associated with specific economic cycles or market conditions.

Integrating cryptocurrencies into a traditional asset portfolio requires a thoughtful strategy.

Start by determining what percentage of your portfolio you feel comfortable allocating to digital assets. This decision should reflect your risk tolerance and investment goals.

Some might choose a conservative 5% allocation, while others might feel comfortable with up to 20%, given the potential for high returns.

Periodic rebalancing is crucial to maintain your desired asset distribution. As the value of your investments fluctuates, this practice ensures that no single asset class dominates your portfolio, keeping your risk in check.

Rebalancing might involve selling some appreciated assets or buying more of those underperforming, aligning your portfolio with your strategic goals.

Leveraging modern tools and platforms can be very helpful in effectively managing a mixed-asset portfolio.

Robo-advisors, for instance, offer automated rebalancing services, using algorithms to adjust your asset allocation based on predefined criteria.

These digital advisors are particularly useful for investors who prefer a hands-off approach, ensuring your portfolio remains aligned with your objectives without constant oversight.

Most investment companies offer robo-advisors, so if you have one you currently work with, you can ask them if they offer this service.

Portfolio tracking apps, equipped with crypto support, provide real-time insights into your investments, helping you make informed decisions.

These apps can track performance, analyze trends, and even offer alerts for buying or selling opportunities, giving you the tools to manage your investments efficiently.

Diversifying Your Portfolio with Digital Assets

Incorporating digital assets alongside traditional investments opens the door to unique growth opportunities.

Digital assets are often at the cutting edge of technology, offering exposure to advancements that can redefine industries.

Think of them as tickets to the forefront of financial innovation, where new products and services are constantly being developed.

This access can lead to outsized returns, especially in rapidly growing markets where early adopters often reap significant rewards.

By including digital assets in your portfolio, you can benefit from these potential gains while staying informed about technological trends that could impact other investments.

Setting allocation limits for high-risk crypto projects is a prudent approach. By capping the amount invested in riskier assets, you protect your portfolio from severe downturns.

As we move forward, we'll explore the psychology of investing, focusing on the emotional aspects of decision-making and how to cultivate a resilient mindset in the ever-evolving world of finance.

Psychology of Investing

Imagine standing on a crowded street, where the air buzzes with excitement. Everyone around you is discussing the latest trend, and you feel an almost irresistible urge to join in.

This is the essence of FOMO, or the "Fear of Missing Out," a powerful force that can drive even the most level-headed investors to make rash decisions.

FOMO is a common pitfall in cryptocurrency that can lead to impulsive buying and inflated asset prices.

It's a phenomenon fueled by social media and hype cycles, where a rapid flow of information creates a sense of urgency.

We've all seen it—when a sudden buzz on platforms like Twitter or Reddit sends prices soaring, sometimes based on little more than speculation.

Social media acts as an amplifier, too, turning whispers into roars. It's easy to get excited, especially when everyone seems to be making money.

Herd behavior takes over, pushing prices higher as more people jump in, afraid of being left behind.

But what happens when the excitement fades? Often, those who bought in at the peak are left holding the bag, facing inflated prices that might not reflect the asset's actual value.

This cycle can lead to anxiety and regret, emotions that cloud judgment and can have lasting financial impacts.

The consequences of FOMO are not just financial; they can profoundly affect your mental well-being, leading to stress and a disconnect from family and friends.

Maintaining discipline and resisting the urge to follow the crowd is crucial.

One effective strategy is setting predefined investment rules that align with your financial goals and risk tolerance. These rules act as guardrails, preventing you from making impulsive decisions driven by emotion rather than logic.

Practice patience and maintain a long-term vision, focusing on the bigger picture rather than short-term fluctuations. This mindset can help you avoid the trap of buying high and selling low.

Conduct thorough research and rely on trusted media sources to guide your decisions, ensuring you understand the assets you're investing in and the market cycles they follow.

Panic selling is another emotional trap that can undermine your investment strategy. It's a reaction to sudden market downturns, where fear takes over and prompts hasty decisions to sell at a loss.

This often results in realizing losses that you could have avoided with a more measured approach.

The triggers for panic selling are varied, from negative news reports to abrupt price drops. Still, the outcome is often the same—selling under pressure and missing out on potential recoveries.

Understanding these triggers can help you recognize when you're reacting emotionally rather than strategically.

Managing stress and maintaining composure during volatile market conditions is vital.

Incorporating mindfulness and meditation practices into your routine can help you stay grounded. Techniques like deep breathing or stepping back from the screen can provide clarity and reduce impulsive reactions.

Developing a support network of fellow investors, friends, or family members can offer emotional guidance and perspective. Sharing experiences and discussing strategies with others can help you process your feelings and make more rational decisions.

Mindfulness in Investing

- **Practice Daily Mindfulness:** Incorporate short meditation sessions to help clear your mind and focus on long-term goals.

- **Set Clear Investment Rules:** Write down your predefined rules and review them regularly to keep emotions in check.

- **Build a Support Network:** Identify trusted individuals you can turn to for advice and encouragement during market turbulence.

Remember, investing is as much about managing emotions as it is about choosing the right assets.

By understanding the psychological aspects of investing and implementing strategies to maintain discipline, you can navigate the crypto market more effectively.

This chapter aims to equip you with the tools to recognize and manage emotional triggers, ultimately leading to more informed and confident investment decisions.

Developing a Resilient Investor Mindset

Picture yourself standing firm, like a lighthouse weathering a storm, unyielding to the chaos around you. This is resilience in the world of investing.

In the volatile seas of cryptocurrency, a resilient mindset is your anchor. It helps you navigate the unpredictable tides and remain calm when the waters get rough.

This resilience starts with accepting the inherent risks of cryptocurrency. You must understand that volatility is part and parcel of the crypto landscape.

Markets will rise and fall, sometimes dramatically, and staying informed and adaptable is crucial.

Being informed means keeping up with market trends and news, but adaptability is about responding wisely to changes rather than reacting out of fear or excitement.

Resilient investors share certain traits that set them apart.

Patience is a key characteristic. It's about being able to wait for the right opportunities rather than rushing into decisions.

Perseverance is equally essential. It's the determination to stick to your plan even when the market doesn't go your way.

Flexibility in adapting strategies is another hallmark of resilience. The market is ever-changing, and what worked yesterday might not work tomorrow.

Being open to adjusting your approach ensures you remain relevant and effective.

Successful investors understand that rigid strategies can lead to missed opportunities or unnecessary losses.

Building mental toughness and confidence is not just a one-time effort but a continuous practice.

Start by setting realistic goals and expectations. This approach helps you avoid the disappointment that comes from chasing unrealistic returns.

Instead, focus on achievable milestones that align with your broader financial objectives.

Learning from past experiences is also invaluable. Review your past trades and investments, noting what worked and what didn't.

This reflection provides feedback that can guide future decisions.

Another way to reduce stress is by building a diversified investment strategy. Diversification spreads risk across different assets, cushioning you from the impact of any single asset's poor performance.

Continuous learning and self-improvement play a crucial role in bolstering your resilience.

The crypto world is dynamic, with new developments emerging regularly. Staying educated keeps you ahead of the curve.

Attend workshops and webinars on crypto investing to expand your knowledge and skills.

Engaging with educational resources and communities can also be enlightening. These platforms offer fresh perspectives and insights that can enhance your understanding of the market.

They provide a space for exchanging ideas and learning from others' experiences. Being part of an active community can offer support and encouragement, which is vital for maintaining a resilient mindset.

Interactive Exercise: Building Your Resilience Plan

- **List Your Investment Goals:** Write down short and long-term goals to keep your focus.

- **Identify Learning Opportunities:** Find one workshop or webinar to attend this month.

- **Reflect on Past Investments:** Analyze one past trade weekly to identify what you learned.

Resilience is not about avoiding challenges but facing them confidently and clearly. It's about knowing that setbacks are temporary and that, with the right mindset, you can get through them successfully.

As you cultivate resilience, remember that it's a journey of continuous growth and learning that will empower you to make better investment decisions and ultimately achieve your financial goals.

Learning from Mistakes: Turning Losses into Lessons

Every investor, regardless of experience, faces mistakes. They're inevitable; accepting this fact is crucial to becoming a savvy investor.

Think of mistakes as the tuition you pay to the school of investing.

Throughout history, investors have made common missteps.

Consider the infamous dot-com bubble of the late 1990s, where many jumped into tech stocks without understanding their true value, driven by hype rather than fundamentals.

Or look at the 2008 financial crisis, where risky mortgage-backed securities led to widespread losses.

These historical examples show that errors are part of the process, offering valuable lessons to those who reflect on them.

Even seasoned investors have their stories.

Take Warren Buffett, who famously invested in Dexter Shoe Company, which turned out to be a significant loss.

He admitted that it was a mistake, but he learned from it and moved on, using the experience to sharpen his decision-making skills.

This willingness to acknowledge and learn from errors sets successful investors apart. It's not about avoiding mistakes altogether but what you do after they happen.

Reflecting on and analyzing losses can transform them into powerful learning experiences.

After a loss, take a step back and examine your decision-making process. Were you influenced by external pressures or emotional triggers?

Identifying these biases can help you make more rational choices in the future.

For instance, if you find that fear led you to sell prematurely, you can work on strategies to manage that fear next time.

Understanding the root cause of your decisions allows you to adjust your approach and avoid similar pitfalls.

Documenting your investment outcomes can be an enlightening exercise. Keeping a journal of your trades and the reasons behind them provides a record to review later.

This practice not only highlights what went wrong but also what went right. By regularly reviewing your journal, you can spot patterns in your behavior and refine your strategies.

It's like having a personal coach guiding you to better performance. Once you've identified the lessons from your mistakes, set new objectives to guide your future investments.

These goals should be informed by your insights, helping you avoid repeating past errors.

Embracing a growth mindset is pivotal in this journey. It means viewing setbacks not as failures but as opportunities to learn and improve.

This perspective encourages adaptability, allowing you to pivot when needed and explore new strategies.

Seeking mentorship from experienced investors can accelerate this growth.

Engaging with those who have navigated similar challenges can provide invaluable advice and support. They can offer perspectives you might not have considered and suggest strategies they found effective.

Learning from others' experiences can broaden your understanding and enhance your investing skills.

As I mentioned in the chapter about Trading Bots, my favorite mentor is Dan Hollings. Still, you can find many different crypto mentors online.

Just ensure you follow someone reputable and knowledge-able.

That's one important lesson I learned when I started my first business 24 years ago - it makes a massive difference if you can find a coach who has been successful at what you're trying to accomplish and hire them to teach you.

It will save you years of failure and help you become prof-itable quickly.

Investing is a dynamic process, full of ups and downs. The key is to remain open to change and continuous improvement.

Markets evolve, and so should you. As you gain experience, your strategies and goals will naturally shift.

Embrace this evolution, using every mistake as a stepping stone to greater success.

In the grand scheme of investing, losses are not the end—they're just part of the journey.

By turning these experiences into lessons, you build a foun-dation of knowledge and resilience that prepares you for future challenges.

In the next chapter, we'll explore future trends in cryptocur-rency, equipping you with insights into the evolving land-scape and how to stay ahead.

Future Trends in Cryptocurrency

Imagine a world where banking and financial services are available to everyone, no matter where they live or how much they earn.

Picture a system where you can lend, borrow, and trade without the need for traditional banks, all with just a smartphone.

This is the promise of **Decentralized Finance**, or **DeFi**, a movement shaking up the financial world as we know it.

DeFi is a bold leap into the future, using blockchain technology to replace traditional financial intermediaries with smart contracts and peer-to-peer networks.

These systems operate autonomously, removing the need for centralized control and allowing users to engage directly with each other.

It's like having a financial marketplace in your pocket, open 24/7, without the usual red tape.

At its core, DeFi is about democratizing access to financial services. Imagine exchanging currencies or securing a loan without ever stepping into a bank.

Platforms like **Uniswap** facilitate decentralized trading, allowing you to swap tokens directly with other users. No middleman is taking a cut; you are interacting directly with the market.

Then there's **Aave**, a platform that lets you lend and borrow cryptocurrencies. It's like having a global bank that operates without borders or bureaucracy. You can earn interest on your assets or take out a loan with just a few clicks.

And let's not forget about **MakerDAO**, which issues stablecoins. These are digital currencies pegged to traditional fiat currencies, providing a stable alternative within the volatile crypto space.

DeFi offers many advantages, but it's not without challenges.

On the plus side, it increases accessibility, giving people in underserved regions access to financial tools that were previously out of reach. It's a boon for financial inclusion, leveling the playing field for millions worldwide.

However, the reliance on smart contracts brings its own set of risks. These contracts are only as good as the code they're written on, and those with malicious intent can exploit vulnerabilities.

The decentralized nature of these platforms also raises security concerns, as there's no central authority to rectify errors or compensate for losses.

The impact of DeFi on global finance is profound and multifaceted. It's compelling financial markets to rethink traditional approaches and adapt to new technologies.

Regulatory bodies grapple with overseeing these decentralized systems, which often operate outside conventional frameworks. There's a growing consensus that regulation is needed to ensure consumer protection and stability.

Yet, the challenge lies in creating rules that don't stifle innovation. It's a delicate balance that regulators worldwide are still trying to figure out.

For instance, the concept of "embedded supervision," where regulatory tools are integrated within blockchain systems, is gaining traction as a potential solution.

Exercise: Examining the DeFi Landscape

- **Explore a DeFi Platform:** Choose one DeFi platform (e.g., Uniswap, Aave, or MakerDAO) and spend an hour exploring its features. Note what stands out to you.

- **Consider Accessibility:** Reflect upon how DeFi could improve access to financial services for those in remote or underserved areas. What impact could this have on a global scale?

- **Evaluate Risks:** Identify potential vulnerabilities in DeFi platforms and consider strategies to mitigate these risks.

DeFi is not just a passing trend; it's a transformational force reshaping how we think about money and finance.

Its rise offers a glimpse into a future where financial systems are more inclusive, efficient, and equitable.

As you explore this exciting new frontier, keep an open mind and a cautious eye, balancing the opportunities with the challenges.

NFTs and Beyond: New Avenues for Investment

Imagine owning a piece of digital art, a song, or a unique in-game item secured by blockchain technology. That's what **Non-Fungible Tokens**, or **NFTs**, offer—a new way to own and trade digital assets.

Unlike traditional cryptocurrencies like Bitcoin or Ethereum, which are fungible and can be exchanged one-to-one, NFTs are unique.

Each token represents a specific digital asset, and even if two NFTs look similar, they can't be swapped as equals. This uniqueness is what makes NFTs unique.

They serve as digital certificates of ownership and authenticity, using blockchain for verification and provenance.

Every NFT is recorded on a blockchain, creating a permanent, tamper-proof record of its origin and history.

This transparency ensures that when you purchase an NFT, you know exactly where it came from and who has owned it before you.

The world of NFTs is vast and diverse, with applications across multiple industries. One of the most popular uses is in digital art and collectibles.

Artists can create digital works and sell them directly to buyers, bypassing traditional galleries and auction houses.

This not only empowers artists by giving them more control over their work but also allows collectors to own pieces that are genuinely one-of-a-kind.

Beyond art, NFTs have found a home in the gaming industry. Here, they offer gamers the chance to own unique in-game assets, like skins, weapons, or virtual real estate.

These items can be traded or sold, giving players a sense of ownership and investment in the games they love.

The music and entertainment industries are also exploring NFTs to distribute rights and royalties, allowing artists to sell their music directly to fans as exclusive, collectible tokens.

Investing in NFTs can be a thrilling venture, but it's essential to approach it with both enthusiasm and caution.

On one hand, the market has seen some extraordinary high-profile sales, like the digital artist Beeple's work selling for millions.

Such events have captured global attention, making NFTs a hot topic among investors. However, this hype has also led to market speculation, where prices can skyrocket based on trends rather than intrinsic value.

The NFT market is relatively young, so liquidity can be an issue. Unlike stocks or traditional cryptocurrencies, NFTs might not always find a buyer quickly, making it challenging to sell when needed.

Moreover, market volatility is a concern. The value of NFTs can fluctuate dramatically and be influenced by factors such as celebrity endorsements or technological changes.

The NFT space is ripe for innovation, with several exciting trends on the horizon. One such development is fractional ownership, where high-value NFTs can be divided into smaller, tradable shares.

This allows more people to invest in expensive pieces, democratizing access to valuable digital assets.

Another trend is the integration of NFTs with metaverse platforms—virtual worlds where users can interact, socialize, and trade digital goods.

In such environments, NFTs could represent everything from virtual land to custom avatars, expanding their utility and appeal.

Additionally, advances in NFT standards and interoperability are underway to make NFTs more versatile and compatible across different platforms and applications.

As with any investment, staying informed and weighing the potential risks against the opportunities is crucial.

NFTs represent a fascinating intersection of art, technology, and finance, offering a glimpse into the future of digital ownership.

Whether you're an art enthusiast, a gamer, or an investor, NFTs open up new possibilities for engaging with the digital world in ways that were unimaginable just a few years ago.

If you're looking to buy NFTs (Non-Fungible Tokens), several reputable marketplaces cater to various needs and preferences. Here are some of the top platforms:

- **OpenSea:** Established in 2017, OpenSea is one of the largest NFT marketplaces, offering a vast array of digital assets, including art, music, photography, trading cards, and virtual worlds. It supports multiple blockchains such as Ethereum, Solana, Polygon, Avalanche, and BNB. OpenSea charges a 2.5% fee on every transaction.

- **Rarible:** Rarible is a community-owned platform

where users can create, buy, and sell digital collectibles. It supports multiple blockchains, including Ethereum, Polygon, Solana, Tezos, and Immutable X. Rarible emphasizes decentralization and offers a wide selection of NFTs.

- **SuperRare:** SuperRare is a curated marketplace focusing on high-quality digital art. It features a selective approach, ensuring that each piece meets specific artistic standards. Artists can mint, list, and sell their original works, with a strong emphasis on maintaining ownership and earning royalties from secondary sales.

- **Foundation:** Foundation is an exclusive NFT marketplace for selected artists. To sell NFTs on Foundation, artists must fill out an application and showcase their art portfolio. The platform charges a 5% fee for all sales on both primary and secondary markets.

- **Nifty Gateway:** Nifty Gateway is known for curating high-quality NFTs and features respected artists and brands. Users can take advantage of exclusive drops, and the platform accepts both USD and Ethereum for transactions.

- **Mintable:** Mintable is a gasless NFT marketplace where users can mint memes, audio, or video files into NFTs. The platform is built on the Ethereum and Zilliqa blockchains and charges varying fees depending on the type of NFT.

- **Binance NFT Marketplace:** Operated by one of the largest cryptocurrency exchanges, Binance's NFT marketplace offers a wide range of digital assets. It supports NFTs on the BNB Chain and Ethereum, providing a user-friendly platform for beginners.

- **Coinbase NFT Marketplace:** Coinbase's NFT marketplace features a plethora of blue-chip NFT collections. It allows users to track sales of NFT collections across major marketplaces and enforces NFT royalties.

When choosing a marketplace, consider factors such as the type of NFTs you're interested in, supported blockchains, transaction fees, and the platform's reputation within the NFT community.

Always conduct thorough research to ensure a safe and informed purchasing experience.

Predicting Market Movements: Tools and Techniques

Navigating the unpredictable waters of cryptocurrency markets can feel like trying to predict the weather. Fortunately, we now have advanced tools to help us make sense of these complex systems.

One such tool is **machine learning algorithms**, which project future price movements by analyzing vast amounts of data. These algorithms can identify patterns that escape the human eye, offering insights into potential market trends.

They can provide educated guesses about future market conditions by processing historical data, much like a seasoned meteorologist forecasting a storm. However, they require constant updates and refinement to maintain accuracy.

In addition to machine learning, **sentiment analysis** has become a key method for gauging market mood. This involves sifting through social media platforms, forums, and news articles to detect the collective sentiment of the market.

Think of it as taking the market's emotional temperature. If the buzz is overwhelmingly positive, it might indicate an impending price rally.

Conversely, negative sentiment could signal a downturn. This tool taps into the human side of trading, acknowledging that markets are driven not just by numbers but by emotions and perceptions.

Another invaluable resource is **on-chain data analysis**. This approach delves into blockchain data to reveal real-time insights into market activity.

By examining transaction volumes, wallet addresses, and other blockchain metrics, you can better understand market dynamics.

On-chain analysis provides a level of transparency unique to cryptocurrency, offering a window into the market's inner workings. It's like having an X-ray of the financial system, showing you what's happening beneath the surface.

Artificial intelligence (AI) plays a pivotal role in these predictive technologies. Through **neural networks** and **AI-driven trading bots**, investors can harness the power of AI for automated strategies.

Neural networks mimic the human brain's information processing and can be trained to recognize complex patterns in cryptocurrency markets. This allows them to make predictions with a level of sophistication that traditional methods might miss.

Meanwhile, AI trading bots can execute trades based on programmed strategies, operating around the clock without human intervention. They offer the advantage of speed and precision, potentially seizing opportunities as they arise.

Despite their promise, these predictive tools have limitations. One major pitfall is the over-reliance on historical data.

Countless variables influence markets; past performance doesn't always predict future outcomes.

Additionally, these tools can be sensitive to anomalies or rare events, known as **black swan events**, which can lead to unexpected market reactions.

Relying solely on technology without considering these factors can result in misguided decisions.

To use these predictions effectively, it's crucial to integrate them with a balanced investment strategy.

Combining technical analysis with fundamental insights provides a more comprehensive view of the market—like using both a map and a compass to navigate unfamiliar terrain.

Setting realistic expectations is also key. While these tools can offer valuable guidance, they are not foolproof.

Maintaining a diversified portfolio can help mitigate risks, ensuring you're not overly exposed to any single prediction or market trend.

As markets and technologies evolve, regularly updating prediction models is essential.

Staying informed about the latest AI and machine learning developments can enhance your understanding and application of these tools.

This continuous learning process will empower you to make informed decisions, positioning you to take advantage of opportunities while minimizing risks.

In the ever-changing world of cryptocurrency, these advanced tools offer a way to stay ahead of the curve.

By leveraging predictive technologies, you can better understand market movements, enhancing your investment strategy.

As you explore these techniques, remember to balance technological insights with human judgment, creating a well-rounded approach to investing.

This chapter has provided a glimpse into the future of market analysis, setting the stage for more informed and strategic decisions in the chapters to come.

Building a Sustainable Investment Plan

Have you ever forgotten to write a grocery list, only to find that you end up with a cart full of things you didn't need? Without a plan, investing is like that.

Without clear goals, you might buy assets that don't align with your financial needs or objectives.

Setting achievable financial goals is like mapping out your route before a road trip; it helps guide your decisions and keeps you on track.

This chapter helps you define those goals and ensures they're specific, measurable, and aligned with your plans.

Setting Achievable Financial Goals with Crypto

When venturing into the crypto world, setting clear financial goals is not just beneficial; it's essential.

Think of your goals as a compass, guiding your investment decisions and helping you overcome the often turbulent waters of cryptocurrency.

Establishing specific, measurable goals creates a roadmap for success that keeps you focused and disciplined.

Whether you're saving for a short-term goal like a vacation, a medium-term goal such as buying a home, or a long-term goal like retirement savings, having these targets in mind will shape your investment strategy and ensure your efforts are well-directed.

Short-term goals, for instance, might involve setting aside funds for a dream vacation. With crypto's potential for rapid gains, this could mean investing a small, manageable amount you're comfortable risking.

Medium-term goals, such as purchasing a house, require a more balanced approach, blending riskier assets with more stable investments to protect your nest egg.

Long-term goals, like retirement, provide the luxury of time, allowing you to ride out the market's ups and downs. Here, you can afford to take calculated risks, focusing on diversification and your portfolio's growth potential.

Each goal has its own time horizon and risk profile, so aligning your crypto investments with these factors is crucial.

Aligning your crypto investments with personal goals involves matching your risk level with your time horizon.

Aiming for short-term gains might make you more comfortable with higher-risk investments. But if your focus is long-term growth, a diversified portfolio with a mix of stable and growth-oriented assets might be more suitable.

Establish benchmarks to track your progress, ensuring that your investments are on course to meet your objectives. This could involve setting specific milestones, like reaching a particular portfolio value within a set timeframe, allowing you to adjust your strategy as needed.

You can use several tools and frameworks to set and track your goals.

Financial planning software can help you visualize your progress and make informed decisions.

Programs like **ICONOMI** offer comprehensive portfolio management, allowing you to track your investments across multiple platforms and assets.

Additionally, frameworks like **SMART**—Specific, Measurable, Achievable, Relevant, and Time-bound—can provide structure to your goal-setting process, ensuring that your objectives are clear and actionable.

By incorporating these tools into your strategy, you can maintain oversight and make adjustments as necessary.

Life is full of surprises, and your goals might need to change as circumstances evolve. Flexibility and adaptation are key to maintaining a sustainable investment plan.

Re-evaluate your goals annually, considering any life events like career changes, family growth, or unexpected financial needs.

These events might require you to adjust your strategy, perhaps shifting your focus from short-term gains to long-term stability or vice versa.

Keeping your goals aligned with your current reality ensures that your investment plan remains relevant and practical.

Exercise: Defining Your Crypto Goals

- **Identify Your Goals:** Write down one short-term, one medium-term, and one long-term financial goal.

- **Align with Investments:** Determine how your current or planned crypto investments align with these goals.

- **Set Benchmarks:** Decide on milestones to track your progress toward each goal.

- **Review and Adapt:** Schedule an annual review to reassess your goals and adjust your strategy.

By setting clear, achievable financial goals, you're laying the groundwork for a successful investment journey.

This process helps you stay focused and disciplined and ensures that your efforts align with your broader life plans.

With the right strategy and tools, you can confidently engage with crypto, turning your financial dreams into reality.

Budgeting for Cryptocurrency Investments

In cryptocurrency investing, having a well-structured budget is like having a map. It provides clarity and instills discipline, ensuring you don't wander off into financial chaos.

When you allocate discretionary income for investments, you gain control over your financial path. This means setting aside a portion of your income specifically for crypto, treating it like any other important financial goal.

By doing this, you avoid the temptation to overextend yourself into high-risk assets. Think of it as a safety net, catching you before you fall too deep into the volatile crypto ocean.

Creating a crypto investment budget might sound daunting, but it's straightforward when broken down into steps.

Start by identifying your fixed expenses—those non-negotiable monthly costs like rent, utilities, and insurance.

Next, list your variable expenses, which include groceries, entertainment, and dining out.

Subtract these from your total income to calculate your disposable income. This is the amount left over for savings and investments.

From this, decide how much you will allocate to crypto each month. Set monthly or quarterly investment limits that align with your financial goals and risk tolerance.

This ensures you invest consistently without sacrificing your financial well-being. It's all about striking a balance between being ambitious and being realistic.

Balancing your crypto investments with other financial obligations is crucial for a well-rounded approach.

Imagine your financial life as a table. Each leg represents a different aspect: investments, debt repayment, emergency funds, and insurance. If one leg is shorter than the others, the table wobbles.

There is one exception, though. Consider increasing your debt repayment portion if possible. Prioritizing debt repayment ensures you're not burdened by high-interest loans, which can destroy your financial stability.

Also, maintaining a solid emergency fund acts as a buffer against unexpected expenses, preventing you from dipping into your investments prematurely.

You also want to make sure you have appropriate insurance coverage. Adequate insurance coverage is like an umbrella, protecting you from life's inevitable storms.

Ensuring each leg is sturdy creates a stable base upon which to build your crypto investments.

In today's digital age, several tools and apps make managing your budget straightforward and more efficient.

Personal finance apps like **Mint** and **YNAB (You Need A Budget)** offer intuitive interfaces and powerful features to help you track income and expenses.

Mint provides an overview of your finances, automatically syncing with your bank accounts to categorize spending and highlight areas for improvement.

YNAB, on the other hand, encourages proactive budgeting, helping you allocate every dollar to a specific job.

For those who prefer a more hands-on approach, **spread-sheet templates** (which you can search for on Google) can be customized to suit individual needs, offering flexibility and control.

These digital resources are invaluable in maintaining a clear view of your financial landscape, enabling you to make informed decisions about your crypto investments.

Remember that budgeting is your ally, not your adversary. It provides a framework that supports your financial ambitions while safeguarding against potential pitfalls.

Establishing and adhering to a well-thought-out budget empowers you to invest confidently, knowing you're building a sustainable financial future.

Regular Review and Adjustment of Your Investment Plan

Imagine you're a gardener tending to a plot of land, each plant representing a different investment. Just as plants need water, sunlight, and occasional pruning, your investment plan requires regular attention to thrive.

Regular reviews of your investment plan are like these gardening check-ups, ensuring that your investments are aligned with your financial goals and market conditions.

Setting aside time for quarterly or semi-annual evaluations lets you catch any issues early and make necessary adjustments.

These reviews are necessary to understand how well your investments are performing and whether they still align with your objectives.

During these evaluations, performance metrics and benchmarks become your best friends. They provide a clear picture of how your investments are doing relative to the broader market.

Analyzing portfolio returns and risk levels helps you see the bigger picture.

Are your investments yielding the expected returns? Are you taking on more risk than you initially planned?

Comparing your portfolio's performance against market indices gives context to these questions. It tells you if your investments are on par with the market or trailing behind.

This insight is invaluable for making informed decisions about your next steps.

Once you've gathered this data, it's time to assess your current asset allocation. Rebalancing your portfolio based on performance is crucial to maintaining your desired risk profile.

If one asset class has performed particularly well, it may have grown to occupy a more significant portion of your portfolio than intended.

Rebalancing involves selling a portion of overperforming assets and reinvesting in underperforming ones to maintain a balance that aligns with your risk tolerance and investment goals.

This process is not about chasing the highest returns but ensuring that your portfolio remains diversified and balanced according to your strategy.

The crypto market is dynamic, with new opportunities and technologies emerging regularly. Staying informed about these developments is key to making informed adjustments to your investment plan.

As market conditions evolve, so too should your approach. This might mean adjusting your risk exposure by increasing it to capitalize on growth opportunities or reducing it to safeguard against potential downturns.

Incorporating new investment opportunities, such as emerging cryptocurrencies or blockchain technologies, can also enhance your portfolio's potential.

However, always conduct thorough research and consider how these additions fit into your overall strategy before making changes.

The complexity of these decisions can sometimes be overwhelming, which is why seeking professional advice can be beneficial.

Financial advisors can provide insights into tax-efficient investing strategies, helping you maximize your returns while minimizing tax liabilities.

They can also help you navigate the impact of regulatory changes, ensuring that your investments remain compliant and optimized.

However, it's important to note that most financial advisors are not well-versed in cryptocurrency, as it's still a relatively new and evolving asset class.

If you want advice on incorporating crypto into your investment portfolio, make sure to find an advisor who has specific experience and knowledge in this area.

Consulting with the right professional can bring a fresh perspective to your investment plan, offering tailored advice that aligns with your unique financial situation.

Regular reviews and thoughtful adjustments are the keys to a thriving investment plan. They help you stay on track, adapt to changes, and seize new opportunities.

As we move forward, consider how you can apply these practices to other areas of your financial life. Your financial journey is just beginning, and with the right tools and mindset, the possibilities are endless.

Community and Networking

Forums and social media have become indispensable tools for cryptocurrency investors.

Platforms like **Reddit** have carved out a significant niche, particularly with subreddits like **r/cryptocurrency** and **r/Bitcoin**.

These forums buzz with discussions ranging from market predictions to technical analyses, allowing users to share information and opinions freely.

Reddit's format encourages in-depth conversations, allowing users to upvote valuable content and downvote misinformation, creating a self-regulating flow of credible insights.

It's like a round-the-clock seminar, where you can listen in on discussions, ask questions, and even join debates, all in pursuit of expanding your crypto knowledge.

Twitter, on the other hand, is the fast-paced newsroom of the crypto world. It delivers real-time updates, breaking news, and quick analyses from experts and influencers.

This platform thrives on brevity and immediacy, making it an ideal space to stay informed about the latest market movements and trends.

Following the right accounts can provide a constant stream of valuable information, helping you make timely decisions.

But with the rapid flow of tweets, it's crucial to discern reliable sources from noise. Look for verified accounts and established thought leaders who consistently provide insightful content and engage constructively with their followers.

Then there are **Discord channels**, which have become popular hubs for specific crypto projects. These channels are like virtual clubs where members can explore particular topics, from new coin launches to blockchain development.

They offer a more interactive and intimate setting, often with live discussions and Q&A sessions.

Being part of a Discord community allows you to connect directly with project teams and fellow enthusiasts, fostering a sense of camaraderie and shared purpose.

It's an opportunity to gain insider perspectives and contribute to the project's growth and development.

Engaging in these communities offers numerous benefits. You gain access to diverse perspectives and opinions, which can broaden your understanding and challenge your assumptions.

Participating in discussions helps you learn from others' experiences and insights, enriching your investment strategy.

By asking questions and receiving feedback, you can clarify doubts and refine your approach, making informed decisions more confidently.

However, the vastness of the internet means that not all information is accurate or trustworthy. Developing strategies for identifying reputable sources is essential to explore this landscape effectively.

Start by following verified accounts and known experts within the community. These individuals have built their reputation on credibility and expertise, making them reliable guides in the complex world of crypto.

Additionally, check the historical accuracy of the information shared. Look for consistency in their analyses and predictions, indicating a deeper understanding of the market dynamics.

When contributing to discussions, aim to add value by sharing well-researched information and insights. This not only enhances the quality of the conversation but also helps you establish credibility within the community.

Respect differing viewpoints and maintain civility, even in heated debates. Engaging constructively fosters mutual respect and opens the door to fruitful exchanges of ideas.

By following these best practices, you can effectively participate in community conversations, enriching your knowledge while contributing positively to others' learning experiences.

Exercise: Building Your Crypto Community

- **Identify Two Communities:** Explore subreddits or Discord channels that align with your interests.

- **Contribute Thoughtfully:** Share an insight or question in each community and observe the responses.

- **Evaluate Sources:** Choose a Twitter influencer to follow and assess their reliability by reviewing past content.

Networking with Fellow Investors

Building a network of fellow investors opens doors to collaboration and mutual growth. It's about the information you gain and the relationships you form.

By sharing experiences, you learn from others' successes and mistakes, which can be just as valuable.

The crypto space is vast and ever-evolving, and having a circle of trusted peers helps you navigate it with more confidence and insight.

Finding and connecting with other investors might initially seem daunting, but there are several practical ways to expand your network.

One of the most effective methods is attending cryptocurrency conferences. These events are more than just gatherings; they're melting pots of ideas and innovations.

Picture yourself at a blockchain conference, surrounded by people who share your passion. You're not just listening to keynote speakers; you're engaging in conversations during coffee breaks, exchanging business cards, and forming partnerships for joint ventures or projects.

Each handshake could be the start of your next big opportunity.

If traveling isn't an option, consider joining local or online investment clubs. These groups are excellent for discussing strategies, analyzing market trends, and pooling resources for more significant investments.

This is how I developed my network of crypto enthusiasts with whom I interact regularly, and they've all become great friends.

I've previously mentioned Dan Hollings' course, *The Plan*, and we were all students in that course together.

One of the nice things about these courses is that they usually include a Facebook or Discord group where you can share ideas and learn from others' wins and failures.

The course instructors (cryptocurrency experts) moderate these groups, so you don't have to worry about misinformation.

Well, a group of us started interacting regularly. Now, we constantly message each other with ideas, sharing our best investments and what isn't working for us.

Becoming a part of a group like this helps reduce your learning curve.

Beyond the surface-level interactions, mentorship and peer support play a crucial role in crypto investing.

Having a mentor can be vital. Imagine having someone experienced to turn to when you're unsure about a decision or need encouragement.

A good mentor provides guidance, shares insights from their journey, and helps you avoid pitfalls.

Equally important are accountability partnerships with your peers. These partnerships involve setting goals together, sharing progress updates, and holding each other accountable.

It's like having a workout buddy for your financial goals, pushing you to stay focused and committed.

To maintain and nurture these professional relationships, being proactive is essential. Regularly check in with your network, not just when you need something.

Share progress updates about your investments, celebrate successes, and learn from challenges. Offering mutual support is key.

If you come across an interesting article or a promising project, send it their way.

Collaboration on projects can also strengthen bonds. Working together can lead to new insights and opportunities, whether it's a joint investment or a co-authored blog post.

Remember, networking is a two-way street. The more you give, the more you receive, creating a cycle of growth and support.

Building and maintaining a network of fellow crypto investors is about more than just the transactions or deals you might make. It's about creating a community where you feel supported and motivated and where you can learn and grow alongside others.

This network becomes your sounding board, source of fresh ideas, and safety net in challenging times. As you connect with others, you're not just expanding your knowledge but becoming part of a dynamic, thriving ecosystem bigger than any single investor.

Learning from Influencers and Thought Leaders

In the vast and often turbulent sea of cryptocurrency, influencers and thought leaders stand out like lighthouses, guiding many through the complexities of the market.

These experts have a significant following and have earned their place through keen insights and accurate predictions. Their impact on the community is profound.

By sharing their experiences and knowledge, they shape perceptions, drive trends, and often steer the direction of discussions within the crypto world.

When you follow an influencer, you gain access to a wealth of information that could shape your investment strategies. They offer a lens through which you can view the crypto landscape, providing clarity amid the noise.

One of the most significant benefits of following these influencers is the education and inspiration they provide.

They often have their finger on the pulse of market trends and future developments, offering timely insights that can help you anticipate changes and make informed decisions.

Their success stories and experiences serve as motivation, especially when they share their journey from the beginning.

Seeing how they navigated challenges and seized opportunities can inspire you to approach your investments with a similar mindset.

However, not all influencers are created equal, and evaluating their credibility is crucial before taking their advice to heart.

Start by reviewing their track record. Have they made accurate predictions in the past? Consistent accuracy can be a good indicator of their expertise.

Consider their affiliations and potential biases as well. Some influencers might promote projects or coins because of personal investments or partnerships.

Understanding these relationships helps you discern whether their advice is genuine or influenced by other factors.

Here is a list of some of the most reputable crypto influencers on both Twitter and YouTube:

- **Vitalik Buterin:** Co-founder of Ethereum, Vitalik shares insights on blockchain technology and the future of decentralized systems.

- **Andreas M. Antonopoulos:** Andreas, a well-known Bitcoin advocate and educator, provides in-depth knowledge about Bitcoin and open blockchain technologies.

- **Anthony Pompliano:** An investor and entrepreneur, Anthony discusses Bitcoin, finance, and the digital economy.

- **Michael Saylor:** CEO of MicroStrategy, Michael is known for his strong advocacy of Bitcoin as a treasury reserve asset.

- **Ivan on Tech (Ivan Liljeqvist):** A blockchain educator and developer, Ivan offers daily insights into crypto news and technology.

- **Crypto Finally (Rachel Siegel):** Rachel focuses on cryptocurrency education and mainstream adoption, sharing accessible content for all levels.

- **Crypto Lark (Lark Davis):** Lark analyzes cryptocurrency markets, investment strategies, and emerging blockchain projects.

- **DataDash (Nicholas Merten):** Nicholas covers various topics, including market analysis, trading tips, and cryptocurrency insights.

- **CryptoWendyO:** Wendy offers market analysis, interviews, and educational content to make crypto accessible to everyone.

- **The Moon (Carl Runefelt):** Carl provides technical analysis and market updates, focusing on Bitcoin and other major cryptocurrencies.

- **Coin Bureau**: A popular and reliable channel with a motto to promote the mass adoption of cryptocurrency

- **BitBoy Crypto**: A well-known YouTuber with almost 1.5 million subscribers

- **Brian Jung**: A channel with nearly 2 million subscribers that provides information on blockchain technology and cryptocurrencies

- **Max Maher**: A channel that focuses on finance, investments, and cryptocurrencies

- **Paul Barron Network**: A channel run by author and award-winning journalist Paul Barron

- **Benjamin Cowen**: A channel that provides information on market analysis and trading strategies

- **aantonop**: A channel with over 321,000 subscribers and 758,000 followers on Twitter

These influencers are known for their contributions to the crypto community and for providing valuable insights through their respective platforms.

When making investment decisions, always remember to conduct your own research and consider multiple sources.

Engaging with their content is key to truly benefiting from these thought leaders' insights.

Many influencers host Q&A sessions or live streams, allowing you to ask questions and receive direct feedback.

Participating in these sessions deepens your understanding and will enable you to engage directly with the influencer and other community members.

This interaction can lead to valuable discussions and new perspectives on the topics.

Engaging with their content through comments and discussions is another effective way to gain insights.

You can actively participate in clarifying doubts, expressing your opinions, and contributing to the conversation.

Interacting with others who share your interests is a chance to test your understanding and refine your thoughts.

Additionally, attending webinars or workshops led by influencers can offer a more structured learning experience.

These events often delve deeper into specific topics, providing a comprehensive understanding beyond typical online content.

As you continue to build your knowledge and network, these connections will become invaluable assets in your investment journey.

The upcoming chapter will explore interactive learning and continued education, offering tools and resources to enhance your crypto journey further.

Interactive Learning and Continued Education

In this digital age, various mobile apps offer structured courses, quizzes, and tutorials, making learning about cryptocurrency convenient and engaging.

One such app is **Khan Academy**, renowned for its comprehensive introduction to blockchain technology. With easy-to-follow lessons, it breaks down blockchain mechanics into digestible pieces, making complex ideas easy to grasp.

Another excellent resource is **Coinbase** (one of the exchanges we discussed in a previous chapter), which educates and incentivizes learning through its "Learn and Earn" program.

This initiative rewards you with small amounts of cryptocurrency as you complete educational modules.

Beyond mobile apps, online platforms offer structured courses that deepen your understanding of cryptocurrency.

Coursera's specialization in blockchain and cryptocurrency is one such course that provides a thorough exploration of the field.

The platform offers courses led by university professors and industry experts, ensuring you receive well-rounded instruction.

Meanwhile, **edX's fintech and decentralized finance courses** explore cryptocurrency's broader implications on the financial world.

These courses provide a framework to understand the opportunities and challenges of integrating crypto into traditional financial systems.

For those eager to apply their knowledge in a simulated environment, platforms like **Crypto Parrot** offer invaluable experiences.

Crypto Parrot provides a trading simulator to practice buying and selling without risking real money. This platform allows you to test strategies and gain confidence before entering the live market.

Similarly, sandbox environments offer a safe space to experiment with smart contracts, enabling you to explore blockchain programming without fearing costly mistakes.

These tools are invaluable for building practical skills and understanding the mechanics of the crypto ecosystem.

Selecting the right educational resources is crucial for effective learning.

Start by evaluating user reviews and ratings to gauge the app's reliability and user satisfaction. Look for platforms with a solid reputation and positive feedback from users who share your learning goals.

Consider the depth and breadth of the content offered; a comprehensive platform should cover both foundational concepts and advanced topics, allowing you to grow at your own pace.

Additionally, choose resources that match your preferred learning style, whether that involves watching videos, engaging with interactive modules, or reading detailed articles.

Embracing these educational tools can transform how you approach cryptocurrency. They bring the abstract to life, turning curiosity into confidence, and lay a foundation for informed decision-making in the dynamic world of cryptocurrency.

Keeping Up with Industry News and Updates

The crypto market, notorious for its volatility, relies heavily on news and updates that can influence prices and investor sentiment.

For instance, when China announced its crackdown on Bitcoin mining, the market experienced a significant downturn.

Conversely, regulatory acceptance in other regions, like El Salvador's adoption of Bitcoin as legal tender, can bolster confidence and drive prices up.

Awareness of these developments can help you make informed decisions, allowing you to react swiftly to opportunities and risks.

Staying abreast of innovations in blockchain technology is equally important.

Breakthroughs in scalability, security, and interoperability can affect the value of cryptocurrencies and open up new investment avenues.

For example, advancements in Ethereum's technology, such as the transition to Ethereum 2.0, have significant implications for its network's efficiency and environmental impact.

Keeping an eye on these technological strides ensures you're never caught off guard and can adapt your strategies accordingly.

CoinDesk and **CoinTelegraph** are two stalwarts in the cryptocurrency news space, providing up-to-the-minute updates on market changes and regulatory developments.

Their articles cover various topics, from price analyses to interviews with industry leaders, ensuring you comprehensively understand the market.

For those who prefer a focus on analysis, **The Block** offers in-depth research and insights that help you understand the implications of various trends and decisions.

Podcasts add another dimension to your news intake, allowing you to hear directly from experts.

Shows like **"Unchained"** and **"The Pomp Podcast"** feature interviews with key figures in the crypto world, offering perspectives that might not always make it into written articles.

Integrating news consumption into your daily routine doesn't have to be a chore.

Start by subscribing to newsletters and alerts from your favorite crypto news sources. This way, updates come directly to your inbox, and you can quickly scan through the headlines during a coffee break or commute.

Allocate specific times to catch up on the news, perhaps in the morning or evening, making it a regular habit like brushing your teeth.

This structured approach ensures you stay informed without feeling overwhelmed by the constant influx of information.

When evaluating the credibility of news sources, it's essential to be discerning. The crypto world is rife with misinformation and hype, so always cross-reference information from multiple sources.

If a piece of news seems sensational or too good to be true, check whether other reputable outlets are reporting the same story.

Consider the reputation and track record of the authors or journalists. Have they consistently provided accurate and insightful information in the past?

This due diligence helps you filter out noise and focus on what truly matters.

As we transition into the next chapter, we'll explore how mastering the art of holding onto your investments—known as HODLing—can be a powerful strategy for achieving long-term success.

Mastering the Art of HODLing

When you think about investing, especially in volatile markets like cryptocurrency, it's easy to imagine it as riding a roller coaster. There are thrilling highs and daunting lows.

The term **"HODL"** comes from a famous Bitcoin Forum post where "hold" was misspelled during a market panic, sparking a movement.

It embodies the strategy of holding onto your digital assets through the ups and downs, believing they will appreciate over time.

This philosophy is rooted in patience and the long-term vision that has rewarded those who've held Bitcoin and Ethereum through their historic surges.

Bitcoin's climb from a few cents to tens of thousands of dollars demonstrates the potential gains of a steadfast approach.

Ethereum, too, has shown remarkable growth, especially with its innovations in decentralized applications and smart contracts.

Patience and discipline are your allies when HODLing. It's about resisting the impulse to sell during market dips.

Remember, seasoned investors have weathered these storms by setting predefined time horizons, ensuring they aren't swayed by short-term volatility.

They understand market cycles, acknowledging that down-turns are natural, often followed by recoveries.

This perspective helps maintain composure and shield your emotional well-being from the market's fickle nature.

Learning from these veterans can guide you; they've often overcome the same nervousness, ultimately finding calm in a sea of uncertainty.

Maintaining a strong HODL position requires actionable strategies.

Consider automating your investments through **dollar-cost averaging**. This means putting a fixed amount into your chosen cryptocurrency at regular intervals, reducing the impact of market volatility.

Diversification is another key strategy. By spreading your investments across various assets, you can soften the emotional roller coaster of watching a single investment rise and fall.

This approach stabilizes your portfolio and opens opportunities for growth in different sectors of the crypto market.

Exercise: Strengthening Your HODL Strategy

- **Set a Time Horizon:** Decide on a time frame you're comfortable holding your investments, whether it's one year, five years, or more.

- **Automate Investments:** Consider setting up a plan to automatically invest a fixed amount regularly.

- **Diversify Holdings:** Review your crypto portfolio to ensure a good mix of assets for stability and growth potential.

HODLing offers both portfolio stability and potential for growth.

By holding long-term, you minimize transaction fees and tax implications.

The potential for compounded growth over time makes this a lucrative strategy for those willing to wait.

While the market's fluctuations might test your resolve, the rewards for patience and discipline could be significant.

Evaluating Your Portfolio: When to Hold, When to Sell

When looking at your crypto portfolio, think of it as tending to a garden, where each asset is a plant that needs care and attention. To evaluate their health, you'll want to understand key performance metrics like **ROI (Return on Investment)** and **CAGR (Compound Annual Growth Rate)**:

ROI measures how much you've gained (or lost) compared to your initial investment. To calculate ROI:

$$ROI = \left(\frac{\text{Current Value of Investment} - \text{Initial Investment}}{\text{Initial Investment}} \right) \times 100$$

For example, if you invested $1,000 in Bitcoin and it's now worth $1,500, your ROI is 50%.

CAGR shows the average annual growth rate of your investment, smoothing out the ups and downs of the market. To calculate CAGR:

$$CAGR = \left(\frac{\text{Ending Value}}{\text{Beginning Value}} \right)^{\frac{1}{\text{Number of Years}}} - 1$$

For instance, if your $1,000 investment grew to $1,500 over 3 years, your CAGR is about 14.47% annually. Calculating the CAGR has always been a challenge for me, so if you are the same, you can visit the Resources Page at ArthurBellBooks. com/crypto.html for a link to a free CAGR Calculator.

By comparing these metrics to the overall market performance or other assets in your portfolio, you can assess whether your investments are thriving or underperforming.

This insight is crucial for deciding whether to stay the course or make adjustments to your strategy.

Deciding whether to hold or sell isn't just about numbers. Look for changes in project fundamentals, like shifts in the development team or deviations from the original roadmap, which might signal a need for reassessment.

Keep an eye on regulatory developments, too. New laws or government actions can impact specific assets, potentially altering their long-term viability.

These indicators are like weather forecasts, helping you decide whether to stick with a project or move on to greener pastures.

A clear understanding of these elements allows you to make informed decisions rather than react emotionally to market fluctuations.

It's important to remember that cryptocurrency markets operate in cycles, often spanning around four years.

Historically, the market tends to experience a **bull run**—a period of rapid price increases—following each U.S. presidential election, typically lasting for about a year.

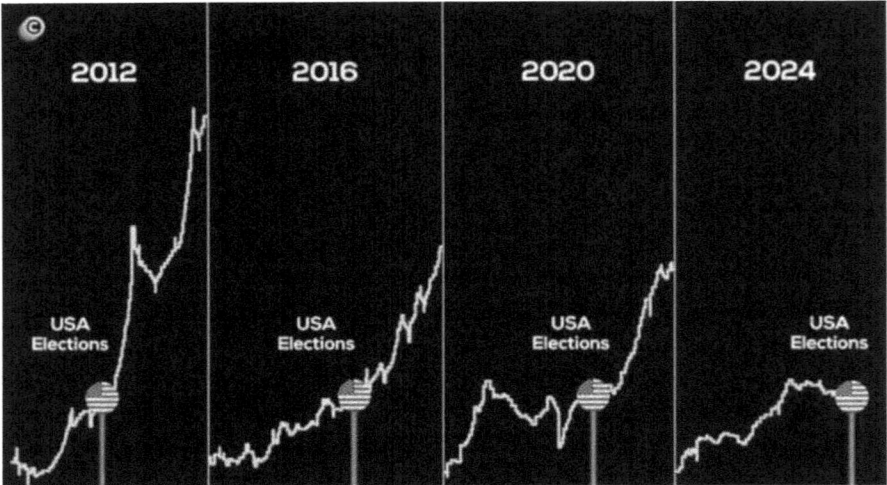

During these cycles, the best opportunities to buy often oc-cur during market downturns, while the optimal time to sell is during the market's upward surge.

Patience is key. Don't rush to sell your assets if they haven't increased in value within a week or a month.

These assets often take time to grow, and reacting too quick-ly could mean missing out on substantial gains later.

Constructing a strategy for selling is as vital as knowing when to buy. Set target prices for each asset where you're com-fortable taking profits.

Consider stop-loss levels, too—points where you'll sell to prevent further losses if the market turns against you.

Reallocating funds from underperforming assets to new op-portunities or safer investments can rejuvenate your portfo-lio.

By combining thoughtful planning with an understanding of market cycles, you can make investment decisions that are proactive rather than reactive, aligning with your financial goals and risk tolerance.

Remember, patience and strategy can transform challenges into opportunities.

Regular portfolio reviews are your best friend. Schedule them quarterly or semi-annually to adjust holdings and ensure everything aligns with your objectives.

This routine helps keep your strategy fresh and responsive to market changes.

Consulting a financial advisor for significant decisions can also provide valuable insights, offering a different perspective that can guide you through complex markets.

Building Confidence as a Crypto Investor

Confidence empowers you to make clear decisions and reduces the anxiety often accompanying volatile markets.

When you believe in your strategy, you're less likely to fall prey to emotional trading.

Instead of reacting to every dip, you can withstand market downturns with poise, understanding that fluctuations are a natural part of the investment landscape.

Confidence helps you keep your eyes on the prize, focusing on long-term goals rather than short-term noise. This mindset is crucial for navigating the ups and downs of the crypto world, where volatility is a constant companion.

Building and maintaining this confidence requires dedication. Continuous education is key; the more you learn, the more equipped you are to make informed decisions.

Explore the resources I discussed previously in this book that expand your knowledge and skills through books, courses, or online forums.

Your confidence will naturally blossom as you grow, making you more resilient to market swings and investment challenges.

Confident investors exhibit certain behaviors that set them apart.

They adhere consistently to a well-defined investment plan, demonstrating discipline and foresight.

Their decisions are calculated and rooted in thorough research rather than impulse. They're willing to take risks only when data and sound judgment back those risks.

This balance between caution and courage defines a successful investor who navigates the crypto seas with assurance and calm.

Celebrating Milestones: Recognizing Your Achievements

Celebrating your achievements boosts motivation and reinforces the positive behaviors that got you there.

Achieving significant profit or witnessing your portfolio grow validates your strategies and efforts.

Take a moment to reflect on how far you've come, the lessons you've learned, and the personal development that has accompanied your financial successes.

Celebration doesn't need to be extravagant, but it should be meaningful.

Whether you treat yourself to something special or take a day off to enjoy your success, the key is acknowledging and appreciating your hard work.

Celebrations can remind you of your progress and potential, motivating you to continue pushing forward.

You can also share your achievements with family and friends. Their support can add a layer of joy to your accomplishments.

However, be selective about who you share your successes with. More people than you might expect would rather see you fail than celebrate your wins.

When I started investing in crypto, I excitedly shared what I was learning and doing with friends and family. More often than not, I heard responses like, "Just be careful. That sounds like a scam to me."

People usually don't understand crypto, and many are afraid of it.

If you want to share your successes, do so with people who genuinely support you and want to see you thrive.

Once you've celebrated, it's time to set new goals. Continuous goal-setting is essential for maintaining momentum.

Establish new financial objectives that challenge you to grow and expand your knowledge in areas like emerging technologies or advanced trading strategies.

This forward-thinking approach keeps your investing journey dynamic and engaging, ensuring you remain adaptable in the ever-evolving crypto landscape.

Setting fresh targets after reaching milestones ensures you continuously move towards new horizons, keeping your investment strategy vibrant and aligned with your long-term vision.

Some achievements deserve special recognition. Perhaps you've reached a specific net worth target or navigated a bear market without succumbing to fear-based decisions.

These milestones are testaments to your dedication and skill. Acknowledging them enhances your journey and prepares you for future challenges, equipping you with the confidence and experience needed to face whatever comes next.

Charting Your Path to Financial Freedom

Congratulations! You've taken the first and most crucial step toward understanding cryptocurrency investing.

But knowledge is only as valuable as what you do with it. Now, it's time to turn what you've learned into action.

The crypto market might seem intimidating, but remember: every expert started as a beginner.

What separates success from hesitation is the willingness to take that first step.

Set up your first account on an exchange, buy your first cryptocurrency—even if it's a small amount—and experience the process firsthand.

This is how you build confidence and truly understand the mechanics of investing.

Don't overthink it. Start simple. Begin with a coin you're comfortable with—perhaps Bitcoin or Ethereum—and use what you've learned to guide your decisions.

Set a budget that aligns with your financial goals, knowing that cryptocurrency is just one piece of your broader financial strategy.

Whether you plan to trade actively or HODL for the long term, the key is to take that first step.

Adopt a Learning Mindset

The world of cryptocurrency is dynamic, and there's always more to explore. New trends, tools, and technologies emerge constantly, and staying informed is crucial.

Don't be afraid to make mistakes—they're part of the learning process. Each decision, trade, or even misstep will teach you something valuable.

Surround yourself with resources and supportive communities. Engage with other investors, join online forums, or attend crypto meetups.

The more you immerse yourself, the more confident and informed you'll become.

Action Items to Get Started

1. **Set up your wallet**: Choose a secure wallet for storing your crypto.

2. **Pick an exchange**: Research and select an exchange that fits your needs.

3. **Make your first trade**: Buy a small amount of cryptocurrency and track its performance.

4. **Practice trading**: Experiment with small amounts to get comfortable with different order types like market and limit orders.

5. **Reflect on your goals**: Decide whether you're in this for short-term gains, long-term growth, or a mix of both.

You're Ready

The cryptocurrency revolution is happening now, and you're equipped to be part of it.

By taking action today, you're not just investing in digital assets—you're investing in yourself.

Patience, persistence, and a willingness to learn will carry you forward.

Imagine looking back in a year or two, confident that you didn't just sit on the sidelines—you participated, grew, and seized opportunities.

The future of finance is here, and it's waiting for you to claim your place in it.

So, take that first step today. The tools are in your hands, and the possibilities are endless.

Here's to your success in the exciting world of cryptocurrency investing!

Fuel the Crypto Revolution

Now that you have the tools and knowledge to invest in cryptocurrency confidently, it's time to inspire others to start their journey.

By sharing your honest opinion of this book on Amazon, you'll help others like you discover the information they need to participate in the crypto world, avoid costly mistakes, and build wealth safely.

Your review is more than just feedback; it guides new readers, showing them where to find the help they want and empowering them to take control of their financial future.

Why Your Review Matters

The world of cryptocurrency grows stronger when knowledge is shared.

By leaving a review, you're not just helping me—you're helping to keep the spirit of innovation and financial independence alive.

Scan the QR code to leave your review on Amazon.

Thank you for being part of this exciting journey. Your voice matters, and your support means the world to me and the growing community of crypto investors.

Let's keep the momentum going and inspire the next wave of cryptocurrency pioneers!

Arthur Bell

References

Bitcoin: A Peer-to-Peer Electronic Cash System https://bitcoin.org/bitcoin.pdf

Using blockchain to drive supply chain transparency https://www2.deloitte.com/us/en/pages/operations/articles/blockchain-supply-chain-innovation.html

Understanding the Impact of Cryptocurrency on Traditional ... https://www.fintechweekly.com/magazine/articles/understanding-the-impact-of-cryptocurrency-on-traditional-banking-practices

History of Crypto: A timeline of events that shaped the ... https://cointelegraph.com/news/history-of-crypto-introduction

Best Cryptocurrency Wallets of 2024: Guide to Security https://www.businessinsider.com/personal-finance/investing/best-bitcoin-wallet

Best Crypto Exchanges and Apps for December 2024
https://www.investopedia.com/best-crypto-exchanges-5071855

How to Set Up a Crypto Exchange Account
https://www.cryptovantage.com/guides/setting-up-crypto-exchange-account/

Cryptocurrency Wallet Security: Best Practices and Tips
https://www.rapidinnovation.io/post/cryptocurrency-wallet-security-best-practices-and-tips

The Crypto Market Cap: A Guide for Beginners - Coursera
https://www.coursera.org/articles/crypto-market-cap#:~:text=Simply%20put%2C%20the%20crypto%20market,coins%20are%20currently%20in%20circulation.

15 Cryptocurrency Forecasts For 2025
https://investinghaven.com/crypto-forecasts/15-cryptocurrency-forecasts-2025/

What is the Bitcoin Rainbow Chart and How It Works?
https://coinbureau.com/education/bitcoin-rainbow-chart/

The 2025 Guide to Crypto Portfolio Diversification - Block-Guard
https://www.blockguard.org/blog/crypto-portfolio-diversification-guide

Short-term vs. Long-term Crypto Investment Strategies [2024] https://www.iconomi.com/blog/short-term-vs-long-term-crypto-investing

How to Create a Well-Balanced Crypto Portfolio
https://www.fool.com/investing/stock-market/market-sectors/financials/cryptocurrency-stocks/crypto-portfolio/

What Charts Should Crypto Investors Use?
https://www.investopedia.com/charts-for-crypto-6500665

20 Best Cryptocurrency Trading Strategies 2024
https://www.quantifiedstrategies.com/cryptocurrency-trading-strategies/

Crypto Security: Best Practices To Protect Digital Assets
https://trakx.io/resources/insights/crypto-security/

Cryptocurrency Scams: How to Spot, Report, and Avoid Them
https://www.investopedia.com/articles/forex/042315/beware-these-five-bitcoin-scams.asp

Best Risk Management Strategies for Crypto Investors
https://www.tokenmetrics.com/blog/risk-management-strategies

Understanding the Security Model of Hardware Wallets
https://davidveksler.substack.com/p/understanding-the-security-model#:~:text=Hardware%20wallets%20also%20referred%20to,such%20as%20hacking%20and%20phishing.

The 10 Best Crypto Trading Bots in 2024 (Reviewed)
https://coinledger.io/tools/best-crypto-trading-bots

Secure Storage of Crypto Assets: Guide to Setting up Cold ...
https://droomdroom.com/how-to-set-up-a-cold-wallet/

Top Crypto Communities to join in 2024
https://coingape.com/crypto-communities/

Cryptocurrency Scams: How to Spot, Report, and Avoid Them
https://www.investopedia.com/articles/forex/042315/beware-these-five-bitcoin-scams.asp

Crypto regulation: key updates and developments (Dec 2024)
https://www.lexology.com/pro/content/crypto-regulation-key-updates-and-developments-dec-2024#:~:text=On%2023%20October%202024%2C%20the,states%20to%20establish%20crypto%20regulatory

Crypto Taxes: The Complete Guide (2024)
https://coinledger.io/guides/crypto-tax

Cryptocurrencies as part of responsible investing
https://www.northcrypto.com/learn/blog/cryptocurrencies-as-part-of-responsible-investing

UN Study Reveals the Hidden Environmental Impacts of ...
https://unu.edu/press-release/un-study-reveals-hidden-environmental-impacts-bitcoin-carbon-not-only-harmful-product

Who is Erik Finman, the Bitcoin Millionaire Teenager?
https://www.investopedia.com/news/who-erik-finman-bitco

in-millionaire-teenager/#:~:text=In%20May%20of%202011
%2C%20at,into%20an%20impressive%20%241%20million.

BitConnect Founder Indicted in Global $2.4 Billion ...
https://www.justice.gov/opa/pr/bitconnect-founder-indicte
d-global-24-billion-cryptocurrency-scheme

The Role of Cryptocurrency in Enhancing Financial Inclusion
https://evertas.com/news/the-role-of-cryptocurrency-in-en
hancing-financial-inclusion/#:~:text=Cryptocurrencies%20a
re%20increasingly%20viewed%20as,relying%20on%20tradi
tional%20banking%20infrastructures.

Real-World Use Cases for Smart Contracts and dApps - Gem-
ini
https://www.gemini.com/cryptopedia/smart-contract-exam
ples-smart-contract-use-cases

Buying Crypto With IRAs: Bitcoin IRAs & Crypto IRAs | Gemi-
ni
https://www.gemini.com/cryptopedia/bitcoin-ira-crypto-ira
-how-to-buy-crypto-with-ira

Best Bitcoin IRAs: Investing in Your Crypto-Powered ...
https://www.businessinsider.com/personal-finance/investin
g/best-bitcoin-cryptocurrency-iras

Ultimate Guide to Diversifying Your Crypto Portfolio
https://www.honeybricks.com/learn/crypto-portfolio-diversif
ication

Digital Assets: The Next Frontier for Markets and Investors
https://www.ssga.com/us/en/individual/insights/digital-ass
ets-the-next-frontier-for-markets-and-investors

How to Deal with Crypto FOMO - Investopedia
https://www.investopedia.com/deal-with-crypto-fomo-6455
103#:~:text=FOMO%20in%20cryptocurrency%20leads%20p
eople,much%20more%20beneficial%20and%20profitable.

Managing investment emotions: building resilience
https://www.lgt.com/global-en/market-assessments/insight
s/financial-markets/investors-why-managing-emotion-is-cr
ucial-for-maximising-outcomes-198462

Embracing Losses as Learning Opportunities: The Path to ...
https://investwithjacob.com/embracing-losses-as-learning
-opportunities-the-path-to-growth-in-trading/

8 Ways To Use Financial Mindfulness To Enhance Your Life
https://www.forbes.com/sites/financialfinesse/2024/05/07/f
inancial-mindfulness-the-key-to-enhancing-your-financial-li
fe/#:~:text=Techniques%20like%20deep%20breathing%20o
r,translate%20into%20better%20financial%20decisions.

Decentralized Finance (DeFi) and Its Impact on Traditional ...
https://papers.ssrn.com/sol3/papers.cfm?abstract_id=4942
313

6 Top NFT Trends to Watch Out For (2024 & 2025)
https://nftevening.com/6-top-nft-trends-to-watch-out-for-2
024-2025/

The Best AI Crypto Prediction App of 2024
https://www.inciteai.com/articles/the-best-ai-crypto-predict
ion-app

Regulating Decentralized Financial Technology: A Qualitative
...
https://stanford-jblp.pubpub.org/pub/regulating-defi

How to Set 'SMART' Crypto Investment Goals
https://coindcx.com/blog/cryptocurrency/crypto-investing-s
trategy/

3 Best Crypto Asset Management Software Platforms
[2024]
https://www.iconomi.com/blog/crypto-asset-management
-platform

10 Rules of Investing in Crypto - Investopedia
https://www.investopedia.com/investing-in-crypto-6502543
#:~:text=Never%20Invest%20More%20Than%20You%20Ca
n%20Afford%20to%20Lose,-Cryptocurrencies%20are%20sti
ll&text=At%20the%20very%20least%2C%20you,than%205%
25%20of%20your%20portfolio.

Explore the Best Crypto Communities of 2024
https://asicmarketplace.com/blog/best-crypto-communities
/?srsltid=AfmBOop1PsU2m3GOeIvxIvITktqALDKEdNkEEI-z4
GOqVGkC2mNg1WKU

The #1 Guide to Blockchain Events and Conferences in 2024
https://www.bizzabo.com/blog/blockchain-events

10 Crypto Influencers You Should Be Following
https://www.investopedia.com/crypto-influencers-you-shou
ld-follow-5224141

5 Tips For Researching And Analyzing A Cryptocurrency
https://www.bankrate.com/investing/researching-and-anal
yzing-crypto/

10 Best Learn and Earn Crypto Programs December 2024
https://koinly.io/blog/learn-and-earn-crypto/

Crypto Parrot: Cryptocurrency Trading Simulator
https://cryptoparrot.com/

CoinDesk: Bitcoin, Ethereum, Crypto News and Price Data
https://www.coindesk.com/

Gamification and Gaming in Cryptocurrency Education
https://journals.sagepub.com/doi/full/10.1177/1046878123
1223762

HODL - Overview, History, Benefits and Risks of HODLING
https://corporatefinanceinstitute.com/resources/cryptocurr
ency/hodl/#:~:text=Summary,from%20long%2Dterm%20val
ue%20appreciation.

11 Essential Strategies for Effective Cryptocurrency ...
https://www.businessage.com/post/11-essential-strategies
-for-effective-cryptocurrency-portfolio-management

Crypto confidence is driving institutional investment, study
...

https://funds-europe.com/crypto-confidence-is-driving-insti
tutional-investment-study-finds/

Crypto Mentorship Programs: Are They Worth It and How to
...
https://funderpro.com/blog/crypto-mentorship-programs-a
re-they-worth-it-and-how-to-avoid-scams/

Forbes Advisor. (n.d.). est crypto wallets. Forbes. Retrieved
December 23, 2024, from
https://www.forbes.com/advisor/investing/cryptocurrency/
best-crypto-wallets

CryptoVantage. Best cryptocurrency wallets. Retrieved December 23, 2024, from
https://www.cryptovantage.com/best-crypto-wallets

Finder. Cryptocurrency wallets. Retrieved December 23,
2024, from
https://www.finder.com/cryptocurrency/wallets

Money.com. Best crypto wallets. Retrieved December 23,
2024, from
https://money.com/best-crypto-wallets

Benzinga. Best cryptocurrency wallets. Retrieved December
23, 2024, from
https://www.benzinga.com/money/best-crypto-wallets

About the Author

Arthur Bell has been a thriving entrepreneur and successful business owner for over 24 years.

His journey into the world of cryptocurrency began in 2000, long before it became a mainstream phenomenon.

Since then, Arthur has honed his expertise, achieving re-markable success with multiple investments that have more than quadrupled in value.

With years of experience navigating diverse markets, Arthur has mastered various trading strategies tailored to different conditions, making him a trusted voice in the crypto and business niches.

Through his books, Arthur is committed to sharing his wealth of knowledge, empowering readers to build wealth, and helping them navigate the ever-evolving world of finance with confidence.

www.ingramcontent.com/pod-product-compliance
Lightning Source LLC
Chambersburg PA
CBHW071557210326
41597CB00019B/3290